No BS (Bad Stats)

Personal/Public Scholarship

VOLUME 4

Series Editor

Patricia Leavy (*USA*)

Scope

The *Personal/Public Scholarship* book series values: (1) public scholarship (scholarship that is accessible to academic and popular audiences), and (2) interconnections between the personal and public in all areas of cultural, social, economic and political life. We publish textbooks, monographs and anthologies (original material only).

Please consult www.patricialeavy.com for submission requirements (click the book series tab).

The titles published in this series are listed at *brill.com/pepu*

No BS (Bad Stats)

Black People Need People Who Believe in Black People Enough Not to Believe Every Bad Thing They Hear about Black People

By

Ivory A. Toldson

BRILL

SENSE

LEIDEN | BOSTON

Cover illustration: Photograph by Ivory A. Toldson

All chapters in this book have undergone peer review.

The Library of Congress Cataloging-in-Publication Data is available online at http://catalog.loc.gov

ISSN 2542-9671
ISBN 978-90-04-39702-6 (paperback)
ISBN 978-90-04-39703-3 (hardback)
ISBN 978-90-04-39704-0 (e-book)

This book is printed on acid-free paper and produced in a sustainable manner.

ADVANCE PRAISE FOR
NO BS (BAD STATS)

"As a member of the Little Rock Nine, I know firsthand how racial discrimination and segregation damages schools and harms millions of Black learners. Dr. Toldson is an education activist for this century who skillfully blends academic prose with sharp wit and human sensibilities to challenge wayward thinking and stimulate innovation. We need to stop the BS driving education policy by reading *No BS*!"
– Ernest Gideon Green, member of the Little Rock Nine (1957)

"Toldson brings science, common sense and passion to bear on an issue on which too many of us have given up. To know Black youth is to recognize their ability to learn when given appropriate opportunities. This is a book well worth reading."
– Edmund W. Gordon, PhD, John M. Musser Professor of Psychology, Emeritus, Yale University

"*No BS* is the book the HBCU Community has been waiting for! For those committed to educating students of color, Toldson's intellectually honest, data driven analysis is a breath of fresh air. This seminal work should be required reading for anyone who is sincere about educational access and equity."
– Roslyn Clark Artis, JD, EdD, President, Benedict College

"Ivory Toldson, with his cleverly entitled book *No BS*, is at his best with real talk and real data. He is my numbers scholar. This unique book debunks myths and lies to improve excellence and equity for students of color."
– Donna Y. Ford, PhD, Professor of Education and Human Development, Vanderbilt University

"*No BS (Bad Stats)* is an instant classic! Dr. Toldson masterfully guides the reader through an intellectually invigorating thought-process that debunks the BS (Bad Stats) about Black students to illuminating a pathway for academic success and life transformation. I highly endorse this much-needed contribution to the field of education!"
– Chance W. Lewis, PhD, Carol Grotnes Belk Distinguished Professor of Urban Education, University of North Carolina at Charlotte

"Everything is good about *No BS*. In an era where 'alternative facts' have entered our lexicon, Ivory Toldson lays out the real data, facts and statistics about what's really going on in the Black community. He also provides keen insights and evidenced-based strategies on how to craft an agenda to empower Black students to realize all of their potential. Terrific book!"
– David Wilson, PhD, President, Morgan State University

PRAISE FOR THE AUTHOR

"Dr. Ivory Toldson is a prolific young scholar and myth buster. He has courageously debunked research and media coverage that perpetuates misleading stereotypes about African Americans. And he is a champion of increasing opportunities for black men, including teaching opportunities."
– Former U.S. Secretary of Education Arne Duncan, in speech, The Enduring and Evolving Role of HBCUs
(https://www.ed.gov/news/speeches/enduring-and-evolving-role-hbcus)

"Look deeper into the dispiriting statistics about young black men and boys and you'll find a rarely acknowledged beauty: an indomitable spirit and irrepressible desire to beat the odds. That's what Howard University psychology professor Ivory Toldson revealed."
– Courtland Milloy, *Washington Post*
(https://www.washingtonpost.com/local/young-black-males-in-the-district-are-refusing-to-be-counted-out/2014/06/03/05cfc39a-eb56-11e3-b98c-72cef4a00499_story.html)

"Toldson had another point which was this: This representation of a crisis scenario too often leads to extreme and unhelpful solutions, including a dumbing down of the kinds of educational opportunities that are often directed to black boys, not to mention an ongoing stigma that even the most motivated and excellent students have to fight. He says this refusal to look at the data closely – to prefer a story over the facts – creates more problems than it solves."
– Michel Martin, NPR
(https://www.npr.org/2014/06/11/320997355/do-you-want-the-truth-or-do-you-just-like-your-story-better)

*To the loving memory of my father, Dr. Ivory Lee Toldson,
my stepfather, Dr. Imari Obadele, and my mentor and
friend, Dr. George Cooper*

CONTENTS

ACKNOWLEDGEMENTS

I gratefully acknowledge the people who have directly and indirectly provided me with the support necessary to complete this project.

First, thank you to my wife, Marshella, and my children, Makena and Ivory Kaleb for your enduring love and attention. I'm also thankful for the love and wisdom of my mother Johnita Scott. And thank you to my mother- and father-in-law Janet and Wilbert Atkinson.

Thank you to Patricia Leavy for believing in my message and mentoring me throughout this process. Thank you to my aunt Amatulla El Amin and colleague Katrina Dunn for helping me with editing. I also thank the leadership at Brill Sense including John Bennett my publisher, Jolanda Karada my production manager, and Paul Chambers, head of marketing and sales.

I am grateful to work with supportive and dynamic people who help me to cultivate ideas through collaborations, dialogue and discourse. This includes the faculty and staff at the Howard University School of Education, the staff of The Quality Education for Minorities Network, Laura-Lee, Hassan, Mercy, and Shaunette; and The Journal of Negro Education, Lenda and Cynthia.

Past experiences with national publications, organizations, and foundations also help me to formulate my ideas. For this, I thank: the National Science Foundation; The Root; The Congressional Black Caucus Foundation; The White House Initiative on HBCUs staff Sedika, Elyse, Tammi and Jaye; The National Urban League; the Open Society Foundation Campaign for Black Male Achievement, led by Shawn Dove; The National Education Association; The Manhood Training Village, managed by my loving stepmother, Frances Toldson; the Southern University Psychology Department, chaired by my first professional mentor, Murielle Harrison; my LifeTagger partners, Marlon and Kendrick; and fellow members of Alpha Phi Alpha Fraternity and Sigma Pi Phi Fraternity.

I'm thankful to many thought partners who participated in earlier stages of the research presented in this book. I'm forever grateful to filmmaker Janks Morton who began debunking myths long before me and taught me the art of data interrogation and public provocation. I also thank Brianna Lemmons for her research assistance during the earlier stages of my career. I'm grateful for the support of my professional colleagues: Donna Ford, Yolanda Sealy, Chance Lewis, Jerlando Jackson, Damon Williams, Leon Caldwell, Damon

ACKNOWLEDGEMENTS

Hewitt, Adisa Alkebulan, Andre Perry, Patrick Oliver, Kenneth Anderson, Shaun Harper, and Terri Watson.

The data analyses in this book would not be possible if not for the training I received at Louisiana State University, Penn State and Temple University. I also received transformative professional development from the Michigan Population Center and The Inter-university Consortium for Political and Social Research at the University of Michigan.

My experiences working with students, teachers and school administrators around the nation helped me to gain the perspectives necessary to write this book. I've had particularly meaningful experiences working with New York City Public Schools, Broward County Schools, District of Columbia Public Schools, the Virginia Department of Education, and Maryland Commission on Educational Excellence and Innovation (Kirwan Commission). Thank you to my aunt Cleo Scott Brown for inspiring me to use the voices of Black children in my research. I also thank the educators in my family, my aunt Lucille Toldson Esters, my sister Nicholy, and my cousins Devin and Aisha. I also acknowledge other family members who educate children outside of school settings, including my brother Ivan and sister Kilah.

Thank you for the leadership at Howard University for providing me with the academic environment necessary to produce my scholarship. This includes President Wayne Frederick, Dean Dawn Williams, Chair Kimberly Freeman, and my program director, Shareefah Al Uqdah.

Thank you to the many coffee shop baristas and bartenders who accommodated me while I worked on my book from their tables and counters; especially to the teams at Ivy City Smokehouse, Smith Commons, Busboys and Poets, and the City Club of Washington DC.

Finally, I'm thankful for the guidance of my mentors, my aunt Elsie Scott, Hank Frierson, Kofi Lomotey, Dean Leslie Fenwick, Aaron Stills, Harold Cheatham, A. Wade Boykins, Ronald Braithwaite, Orlando Taylor, Leonard Haynes and Ernie Green of the Little Rock Nine.

PART 1

NO BS (BAD STATS)

NO BS (BAD STATS)

We don't need to close the Black-White achievement gap; we need to deconstruct it.

***

Soul food didn't come from emulating White cooks; Jazz, rock-n-roll, and hip hop didn't come from emulating White musicians; and good Black stats won't come from emulating White scholars. WARNING: I cook my research in a rusty pot, with lots of spice, and serve it ostentatiously on two turntables and a mixer. You can acquire a taste for my tone, or let it offend your sensibilities. I'mma be steadfast with my hustle until they start emulating me.

NUMBERS ARE PEOPLE: THE ACHIEVEMENT GAP AS A SOCIAL CONSTRUCT

My 4th grade teacher labeled me a slow learner. I frequently daydreamed and had difficulties paying attention in class. Learning mathematics was especially difficult because I would create characters and stories from numbers.

I assigned every number a gender and personality. The number one was a baby girl, 2 was a young boy, 3 was a young boy, 4 was a girl, 5 was a boy, 6 was a teenage girl, 7 was a teenage girl, 8 was a man, 9 was a woman, and the number 10 was a man. All of my numbers had a story and relationships with each other, and their stories became more elaborate each day. Eventually, I learned to suppress this peculiar impulse, so I could more efficiently learn math at the pace required in traditional schools.

Today, researchers routinely separate numbers from people. We use deficits statistics, test scores, achievement gaps, graduation rates, and school ratings, without a humanistic interpretation. We also create false dichotomies between qualitative and quantitative research. However, my pattern of relating to numbers as a slow-learning elementary school student was consistent with African-centered learning. In ancient Kemet (Egypt), for example, people learned how to multiply based on one number's relationship to another, rather than by using multiplication tables (Akua, 2012).

When conducting research on Black communities in Philadelphia, W.E.B. Du Bois did more than introduce new research methods. He introduced a new philosophy of research as an integrative and immersive experience, and using people to represent numbers, rather than numbers to represent people. Every number is associated with human characteristics that researchers should not ignore. Behind every statistic, there is a person with dreams, aspirations, fears, and needs. Separating numbers from people allows people to oppress people without conscience or consequence.

> What about to be seen as a person with a name, then POOF, a statistic and to many a shame. – Asa Fludd, 11th grader, from *Breaking Barriers* (Toldson, 2008)

In 2008, I unwittingly conducted Duboisian-style community participatory research. Through happenstance, I was a judge for an essay contest for young Black males, called "A Mile in My Shoes," while conducting statistical analyses of large datasets for my "Breaking Barriers" research on Black males (Caldwell, Sewell, Parks, & Toldson, 2009; Toldson, 2008). While conducting multivariate analysis to understand the lives and experiences of Black males who were doing well in school, and those who were not, I became enamored with the writings of the young Black males who participated in the writing contest. The young Black males wrote about their experiences with parents, teachers, friends, and feelings about their communities and futures. Their perspectives helped me to contextualize my findings related to household composition, peer influences, health behaviors, and perceptions of school.

For one analysis, I used Health Behaviors in School-age Children (HBSC) to examine a wide range of factors that could directly or indirectly measure emotional well-being and self-esteem, including measures of self-worth, psychomotor stressors, and use of psychotropic medication. Using stepwise multiple regression analysis, I found that three factors demonstrated a significant relationship with academic achievement and Black males: (a) quality of life, (b) tired in the morning and (c) feeling lonely. The analysis demonstrated that "quality of life" and academic achievement were positively correlated. The opposite was true of feeling tired in the morning. Black male students who reported being more frequently tired in the morning reported lower levels of academic performance (Toldson, 2008).

Admittedly, beyond the statistical evidence, I did not initially fully comprehend the relationship between being tired in the morning and academic performance among young Black males. However, while rating an essay from "A Mile in My Shoes," I read:

> I think sometimes we don't get enough sleep and can't stay up during class, which affects how much information you get from the teacher. From that you don't take very good notes. Then, you study bad notes and have the wrong information. Now, you take a test and get a bad grade. That gives people further reason to believe that we are dumb and don't know anything. – Brian Bunkley, 8th Grade, from *Breaking Barriers* (Toldson, 2008)

This insightful analysis helped me, as a researcher, to "connect the dots" beyond the x and y coordinates of a correlation plot. Mr. Bunkley helped me to understand a pattern which can originate from home and community disorganization, to a young Black male being unfairly stereotyped at the school by people who are looking for "further reason" to believe that Black students are academically inept. In other words, Mr. Bunkley spoke to the confirmation biases that people use who are hypersensitive to an "achievement gap."

The achievement gap is typically exemplified as a numerical representation of the distance between two races on a specific performance indicator, such as a test score (Chambers, 2009). However, positioning the 'number' as an independent, static representative of an elusive "gap," without considering the human context, allows researchers to facilitate misguided, and often oppressive, actions under a veneer of objectivity (Ladson-Billings, 2007).

"Academic achievement" is a social construct. Indicators of academic achievement are meaningless without their relationship to positive life outcomes. Thus, in theory, indicators of academic achievement (like test scores and grades) should "predict" positive life outcomes. However, in practice, indicators of academic achievement "determine" positive life outcomes.

This is a problem because we can never know if the academic "things" we measure have any real relationship to positive life outcomes. Educators and parents fixate more on "things," like test scores and grades, and neglect fundamental social, developmental, and educational needs that are more important than the "things" upon which we fixate.

The academic achievement "gap" is also a social construct. In theory, we use indicators of the academic achievement gap to "predict" social inequities. However, in practice, we use indicators of the academic achievement gap to help oppressors "create" social inequities. This is a problem.

5

A DUBOISIAN FRAMEWORK FOR EDUCATIONAL EQUITY

In 1899, W.E.B. Du Bois revolutionized social science research by using geocoding, immersive participatory research, archival research, non-deficit research paradigms, and surveys, when he published *The Philadelphia Negro* (Zuberi, 2004). From 1896 to 1897, Du Bois lived in the same neighborhood as his research participants and coded a map of the area to demonstrate the in-group diversity of Black Philadelphians, as well as the complexities and nuances of their needs. His ground-breaking research on Black Americans paved the way for modern, technology facilitated research strategies, such as geographic information system (GIS) mapping and big data analytics (Hunter, 2015).

Du Bois' research demonstrated that complex problems require rich and comprehensive data, sophisticated analyses, and a holistic understanding. His research methods transcended the qualitative versus quantitative dichotomy by integrating qualitative approaches to collecting quantitative data. Figure 1.1 is a proposed framework for using Du Bois' approach to understand and find solutions for educational inequalities.

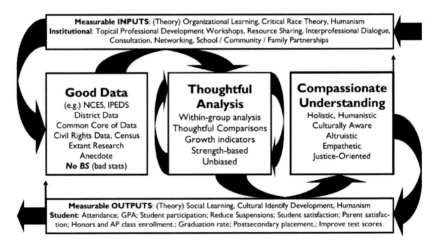

Figure 1.1. A framework for promoting educational equity

Many are familiar with that adage "garbage in, garbage out"; a concept common in mathematics and computer science. "Garbage in, garbage out" describes the process by which the quality of the input determines the accuracy of the output. Applied to educational issues, this saying implies that when resources to address problems are misinformed and misappropriated, the problems will persist or get worse. As demonstrated by the model, the primary source of misinformed inputs in educational research is bad data, thoughtless analyses, and a lack of compassion when interpreting and addressing educational issues. The following sections provide details on how to position information to produce the best educational outcomes for Black students.

Good Data

Good data is comprehensive, holistic, and provide a complete picture of important issues. Many various sources, most of which are publicly accessible, can help us to develop a comprehensive picture. These are popular sources to gather data on educational issues, including access and equity:

- *The National Center for Education Statistics (NCES)* collects and analyzes data related to education in the U.S. Data is publicly available to access and analyze. (https://nces.ed.gov/)
- *The Common Core of Data (CCD)* is the Department of Education's comprehensive, annual database on all public elementary and secondary schools and school districts. (https://nces.ed.gov/ccd/)
- *Civil Rights Data Collection (CRDC)* collects and reports data on key education and civil rights issues in public schools. (https://ocrdata.ed.gov/)
- *American Community Survey (ACS)* of the U.S. Census Bureau is an annual survey of ancestry, educational attainment, income, language proficiency, migration, disability, employment, and housing characteristics. (https://www.census.gov/programs-surveys/acs/)
- *Current Population Survey School Enrollment Supplement* is a national survey on information about school enrollment for household members age 3 and older. It is a proxy response survey sponsored by the National Center for Education Statistics (NCES), Bureau of Labor Statistics (BLS) and the United States Census Bureau. (https://nces.ed.gov/surveys/cps/) (https://catalog.data.gov/dataset/current-population-survey-school-enrollment-supplement)
- *The National Assessment of Educational Progress (NAEP)* is the largest nationally representative and continuing assessment of students' aptitude in specific subject areas. (https://nces.ed.gov/nationsreportcard/)

Importantly, from a DuBoisian framework, researchers do not collect data in isolation from the subject or *unwitting* research participant. An unwitting research participant is a person who has personal, emotional, or social characteristics that match the research population of interest; however, they are unaware of or have no input on the motivations and consequences of the study. Good data is collected in a manner that allows research participants to provide more in-depth information about the statistics being collected and enables the researcher to subjectively connect to the research. This process of "humanizing" the data is essential to good research (Chrisler, 2015). Humanizing data can come from direct correspondence with unwitting research participants, or through augmenting research literature with news articles, blogs, and videos that capture multiple aspects of the lives and experiences of the research study. For Black people especially, we should consider all "objective" and dehumanized studies about Black people as invalid (Toldson, 2018). Studies about Black people, without the perspective of Black people, is BS (bad stats).

In education, gathering proximal data is important to supplement data from large national or district data. The following, shown in Table 1.1, are suggestions for useful proximal qualitative and quantitative data.

Table 1.1. Proximal school-related data to gather comprehensive and holistic information on student achievement

Average attendance	Postsecondary placement
Collective GPA	Percent of students advancing to 4-year colleges
Participation in competitions (science fairs, spelling bees, math competition)	Number of home visits
Suspension rate	Frequency of contact with parents
Student satisfaction surveys	Counselor to student ratio
Curriculum reviews	Teacher to student ratio
Teachers' total number of hours in professional development	Administrative tenure
Teacher's credential and certification	Number of enrichment programs
Percent of students participating in extracurricular activities	Age and quality of textbooks
Percent of students in honors and AP classes	Time using technology
Dropout rate	Time spent participating in laboratory experiences
Graduation rate	Student merit awards given

Good data is open to multiple interpretations. BS masquerade as the interpretation. Good data provides the necessary pieces of information to assemble into a complete picture of the issue and lends itself to data storytelling. After gathering good data, the next step is to provide thoughtful analysis.

Thoughtful Analysis

Within-group analysis and thoughtful comparisons. A thoughtful analysis requires a subjective connection to the data. Several analytics strategies can lead to more meaningful conclusions about the data. Within-group, as opposed to between-group analysis, enables the research to expand and enrich the range of findings for the research population. The achievement gap, for instance, results from between-group analyses that make the erroneous assumption that one group needs measured characteristics that are statistically compatible with another race to achieve equity. This short-sighted view typically positions White achievement levels as a standard for Black students to attain, and masks resilience and unexpected levels of success among Black students. To illustrate this point, using data from the American Community Survey (Toldson & Lemmons, 2015), I once quipped on Facebook:

> Thirty-nine percent of Black children in DC are living in poverty, compared to 0 percent of White children. Ninety percent of White children in DC are from families that are "comfortable," as measured by having an income that is more than five times the rate of poverty, compared to 15 percent for Black children. So, you're telling me that the gap between the percentage of White and Black families who are wealthy is 75, yet the gap between the percentage of White and Black children who complete high school is only 13? What's wrong with White people?

Interestingly, one of the commenters on Facebook accused me of taking a "jab" at White people, which was certainly not my intent. However, we often fail to acknowledge that typical thoughtless analyses that compare Black people to White people, without context, naturally lead to the common question, "What's wrong with Black people?"

If researchers want to determine how Black students can perform at their highest levels in school, they should examine the variance between high-achieving Black students and underachieving Black students, rather than between all White students and all Black students. An exploration of the family, social, and educational strategies of high-achieving Black students should be central to the research, not merely serendipity. Otherwise, the researcher runs the risk of extolling a narrow set of exclusive and elusive strategies, which are only relevant to students and families that have access to restricted social and economic resources. When conducting between-group analysis to study the achievement gap, a researcher could easily conclude that social discrimination is the best way to achieve academic success.

Growth indicators and strength-based analysis. Another common barrier to a thoughtful analysis is viewing data and statistics as static, rather than dynamic. Again, numbers are people; and like people, numbers can improve with time and effort. The objective of research should not be to produce numbers. It is to understand the living conditions that could make the numbers change, as well as to interrogate the data to determine the true level of confidence we should have in the statistics.

Several years ago, for example, I heard a policymaker in Memphis admonish the school system because more than half of the children he represented were behind by the first grade.

"How do you know that?" I asked.

"Because students are tested in kindergarten" he said.

"If kindergarteners in your generations or mine were given the same test, do you think we would have done much better?" I asked. The question miffed him, but he allowed me to elaborate.

I explained the nature of cognitive development in early childhood and the inherent danger in using such measures to predict 1st grade readiness, without considering the child's social and emotional adjustment to school. Overall, the dialogue was constructive, but I remained disturbed by the number of people willing to write off children who don't hit certain benchmarks by a certain time. Months later, I was pleased to read the article: "Knox County Schools to discontinue SAT 10 test for kindergartners" (Absher, 2014). This was a decision of one county, but it was a step in the right direction.

When it comes to educating children, it is never too early, and it is never too late. Today, society is overly sensitive to the "early" part. We often stress the importance of early learning experiences by examining the failures of older students. We say things like, "If a child hasn't mastered 'this' by 'then' he/she will never be able to catch up." We spread fictions about [someone] planning prison construction based on second [or third, or fourth] grade reading (Sanders, 2013).

At the same time, we ignore nonlinear developmental processes. Adults who have become successful after spending many years of their childhood "behind" succeed because someone refused to give up on them; because someone believed in them and made them believe in themselves. They often refer to a "click" – the simple thing that triggered a new outlook and inspired them to press on despite the obstacles ahead. Researchers who study Black educational issues must deploy methods of analysis that will lead to the type of compassionate understanding necessary to meaningfully advance education.

From thoughtless to thoughtful: Why aren't Black students reading on grade level? I once heard a principal of a predominantly Black high school state that no student at her school is reading on grade level. What does "not reading on grade level" mean? To the panelists, it meant these students will go to jail, as one quoted the common fallacy that the number (of prison beds) is based on reading scores, and another made a vague statement about the students not being prepared for life.

Technically, and thoughtfully, it means this for students:

- On a national or state assessment of reading, the students achieved a score that was less than the scores achieved by the norm-reference group of students in the same grade. The calculated score is an estimate that reflects both actual reading ability and random error (e.g., motivation, fatigue, resentment, attentional deficits, etc.). And the unknown true score lies within a range of confidence, which varies based on the validity of the assessment and the testing circumstances.
- *Some* of the students who are not reading on level are missing basic level abilities to recognize and express words and understand the meaning of words. However, this is best assessed through oral reading, not silent examinations. These students will need extra care and attention to learn concepts they should have learned in previous grades.
- *Many* students who are not reading on level, have scores that are full of error (see definition above). They could care less about the tests (and honestly, why should they), or they didn't sleep the night before, or they don't like the educator, and see through the con (they know that you want them to do well because it helps the educator, not the students), or they have attentional deficits (which should be assessed independent

to reading ability). These students need social support, inspiration to be re-engaged with the school, more agency over what they read and how they read it, and to know the educator actually cares about them.

A thoughtful analysis of an "achievement gap" in reading test scores, based on good data and not bad stats, requires the following:

- When educators do not know the specific assessment being used, the circumstances by which the test was administered, and doesn't understand the basic concepts of testing theory, they should not prognosticate the fate of students generally who don't read on grade level;
- When educators have not taken the time to identify the specific students who need to learn basic concepts and are generalizing the needs of all students based on a standardized test, they should not generally prognosticate the fate of students who don't read on grade level; and
- When educators have not taken the time to know, care for and inspire students, and are judging them based on a test, they should not generally prognosticate the fate of students who don't read on grade level.

Beyond a thoughtful analysis, educators need the compassion necessary to stop believing every bad thing about Black students, and simply start believing in Black students.

Compassionate Understanding

Ignorance is a crutch. Educators who lack compassion often use declarative sentences that begin with, "I don't understand." For example, "I don't understand why he can't get to school on time," or "I don't understand why her mama let her out the house looking like that." Educators use "I don't understand" statements to deflect attention away from their own deficiencies or insecurities. Compassionate educators seek to understand. More often than not, they will ask, "Help me understand," to open the dialogue necessary to find the means to help students, families, and communities.

Lack of compassion is rooted in explicit and implicit biases (Gibson, Rochat, Tone, & Baron, 2017). Implicit biases are beyond our conscious awareness; however explicit biases are material thoughts. For example, if someone thinks, "These children from predominantly Black neighborhoods lack the appropriate guidance to be prepared for school, and are likely to perform poorly in my class," he or she is expressing a performance jilting explicit bias.

Research studies connecting implicit biases with racist actions are inconclusive. However, the connections between explicit biases and actions are quite clear. In fact, many educators explicitly state their discriminatory intent. For example, an educator might say:

- "Children at this school can't take AP or honors classes";
- "Just suspend him ... his mama don't care anyway";
- "I'm not recommending her for anything ... she comes in here with an attitude and you know where she gets it";
- "You probably should just apply to community colleges"; or
- "I'm not learning Black history to teach Black students, they need to learn normal history first."

The statements above express intentions that are imprudent, unethical, and possibly illegal; however, bias-driven, uncompassionate dispositions toward Black students and families are normalized in educational environments. Biases and lack of compassion explain the achievement gap between White students at elite private schools and Black students at impoverished public schools. Students at elite private schools and affluent public schools often get the best grades because their teachers have higher expectations of them, admire their communities, and are intimidated by their wealthy parents. Therefore, these students' good grades are more about social privilege, not academic acumen. Contrarily, students at impoverished public schools often get the worst grades because their teachers have lower expectations of them, admonish their communities, and are apprehensive toward their low-income parents. Therefore, these students' bad grades are more about social disenfranchisement, not academic deficiencies.

Developing a compassionate understanding of data requires adopting a world view that is culturally aware and social justice oriented, as well as being empathetic and possessing altruistic interpersonal characteristics. Duboisian researchers can use critical race theory (CRT) and humanism as heuristic frameworks to conceptualize the process by which students of diverse backgrounds learn and develop in the classroom and how educators experience the school environment.

CRT examines White privilege and institutional racism. When viewing a racially diverse school system with the tenants of CRT, a White educator who takes a "colorblind" approach to teaching Black students, and ignores social inequalities, inadvertently promotes a racially prejudiced hegemony (Kohli, 2018). In previous studies, critical race theory has been used to demonstrate instructional techniques to develop agency and activism with students (Knaus, 2009), as well as the dynamic that leads to harsher punitive measures at predominately minority schools (Zirkel et al., 2011).

Researchers should also use a humanistic perspective to explore interpersonal dynamics between educators and students that are conducive to a healthy learning environment. Humanistic psychology holds that for a person to grow and mature, they require a nurturing environment that provides them with genuineness, unconditional positive regard, and empathy (Cain, 2014). Genuineness means practicing openness and self-disclosure, unconditional positive regard is the feeling of acceptance, and empathy is expressed in the ability to listen to and understand. Humanistic theorists believe that both educators' feelings toward their students and knowledge of culture are essential to the learning process (Barr, 2011). Humanistic educators do not separate the cognitive and affective domains; rather they insist that schools need to provide students with a nonthreatening environment, so they will feel secure to learn. Once students feel secure, learning becomes easier and more meaningful (Boyer, 2010).

Developing compassion: "Imma tell ya like this."   I was discussing college promotion in secondary education when an appalled 9th grade teacher told me about a student who turned in an essay using the word "Imma." The teacher thought Imma was the name of a person, but the student wrote "Imma" as a neologism to express, "I am going to."

"Using Imma in a 9th grade essay, what do you believe this says about this child's future?" I asked the teacher. She did not respond.

I continued, "If you, and other teachers, believe that this means she is too far behind to have any reasonable chance of graduating from a competitive college, that's the real problem."

"What did she write after 'Imma'? Imma what?" I asked.

The teacher did not respond and seemed to believe the question was irrelevant.

I continued, "'Imma' signals to me that she was writing a personal essay and was revealing an intention to do something. Understanding what her motivations are, can tell us more about her and future than her misuse of the English language at 14 years old."

We have numerous examples, many from past generations, of those who did not master reading and writing mechanics by high school, but still went on to excel in any given discipline. Our children are too valuable for us to diminish them over something as trivial as using "Imma" in an essay. To increase educational advancement for Black students, educational researchers must: know students and families as humans and not numbers; amplify their voices, instead of silencing them; and seek to understand students as cultural citizens with endless potential.

DISCOVERING THE TALENTED TENTH

The purpose of education should be to reveal talents, not to expose weaknesses. Unfortunately, many Black students only go to school to learn what they do not do well. They learn that they are bad test takers, slow readers, not a "math person," or have a short attention span. Educational researchers' impulse to find faults is rooted in the paradigm of the achievement gap, which conditions us to separate high achievers from low achievers on a uniform measure. Reconditioning educators and educational researchers to discover diverse talents among diverse students would not simply "close" the achievement gap; it would render the nomenclature of the achievement gap irrelevant and obsolete.

W.E.B. Du Bois conceptualized the talented tenth. However, it is dangerous to define the talented tenth by White oppressors' standards. It causes certain Black people, many who have qualities and characteristics that are more acceptable to mainstream society, to feel superior (Stefanizzi, 2010). It separates Black people with the highest dose of traditional education from the Black community and dupes them into believing that their contribution to the betterment of Black people is based on their social position and privilege.

Deconstructing the achievement gap also involves reconceptualizing the talented tenth. In this view, the talented tenth is not about ten percent of the Black community identifying an elite club. It is about everyone in the Black community identifying the gifts that make them unique. The talented tenth is not about ten percent of the Black community doing good for the whole. It is about the whole of the Black community using their unique gifts to make the race stronger. When using a Duboisian framework to deconstruct the achievement gap, we shift from asking, "Are you in the talented tenth," and start asking, "What is your talented tenth?"

REFERENCES

Absher, S. (2014, November 3). KCS board pushes to discontinue SAT-10 testing for grades K-2. *The Knoxville Focus.*

Akua, C. (2012). *Education for transformation: The keys to releasing the genius of African American students.* Conyers, GA: Imani Enterprises.

Barr, J. J. (2011). The relationship between teachers' empathy and perceptions of school culture. *Educational Studies, 37*(3), 365–369.

Boyer, W. (2010). Empathy development in teacher candidates. *Early Childhood Education Journal, 38*(4), 313–321. doi:10.1007/s10643-010-0419-8

Cain, D. J. (2014). Person-centered therapy. In G. R. VandenBos, E. Meidenbauer, & J. Frank-McNeil (Eds.), *Psychotherapy theories and techniques: A reader* (pp. 251–259). Washington, DC: American Psychological Association.

Caldwell, L. D., Sewell, A. A., Parks, N., & Toldson, I. A. (2009). Guest editorial: Before the bell rings: Implementing coordinated school health models to influence the academic achievement of African American males. *Journal of Negro Education, 78*(3), 204–215.

Chambers, T. V. (2009). The "receivement gap": School tracking policies and the fallacy of the "achievement gap." *Journal of Negro Education, 78*(4), 417–431.

Chrisler, A. J. (2015). Humanizing research: Decolonizing qualitative inquiry with youth and communities. *Journal of Family Theory & Review, 7*(3), 333–339. doi:10.1111/jftr.12090

Gibson, B. L., Rochat, P., Tone, E. B., & Baron, A. S. (2017). Sources of implicit and explicit intergroup race bias among African-American children and young adults. *PLoS ONE, 12*(9), 1–18. doi:10.1371/journal.pone.0183015

Hunter, M. (2015). W.E.B. Du Bois and Black heterogeneity: How The Philadelphia Negro shaped American sociology. *American Sociologist, 46*(2), 219–233. doi:10.1007/s12108-014-9249-2

Knaus, C. B. (2009). Shut up and listen: Applied critical race theory in the classroom. *Race, Ethnicity and Education, 12*(2), 133–154.

Kohli, R. (2018). Behind school doors: The impact of hostile racial climates on urban teachers of color. *Urban Education, 53*(3), 307–333. doi:10.1177/0042085916636653

Ladson-Billings, G. (2007). Pushing past the achievement gap: An essay on the language of deficit. *Journal of Negro Education, 76*(3), 316–323.

Sanders, K. (2013). Kathleen Ford says private prisons use third-grade data to plan for prison beds. *Politifact.* Retrieved from https://www.politifact.com/florida/statements/2013/jul/16/kathleen-ford/kathleen-ford-says-private-prisons-use-third-grade/

Stefanizzi, L. (2010). Transcending the urban context: W. E. B. Du Bois and the Black Elite from The Philadelphia Negro to 'the talented tenth.' In A. Carosso (Ed.), *Urban cultures of/in the United States: Interdisciplinary perspectives* (pp. 43–62). Bern: Peter Lang.

Toldson, I. A. (2008). *Breaking barriers: Plotting the path to academic success for school-age African-American males.* Washington, DC: Congressional Black Caucus Foundation.

Toldson, I. A. (2018). In search of Wakanda: Lifting the cloak of White objectivity to reveal a powerful Black Nation hidden in plain sight (Editor's commentary). *Journal of Negro Education, 87*(1), 1–3.

Toldson, I. A., & Lemmons, B. P. (2015). Out-of-school time and African American students: Linking concept to practice (Editor's commentary). *Journal of Negro Education, 84*(3), 207–210.

Zirkel, S., Bailey, F., Bathey, S., Hawley, R., Lewis, U., Long, D., ... Winful, A. (2011). 'Isn't that what 'those kids' need?' Urban schools and the master narrative of the 'tough, urban principal.' *Race, Ethnicity & Education, 14*(2), 137–158. doi:10.1080/13613324.2010.519973

Zuberi, T. (2004). W. E. B. Du Bois's sociology: The Philadelphia Negro and social science. *Annals of the American Academy of Political and Social Science, 595,* 146–156. Retrieved from http://ann.sagepub.com/content/by/year

THE HAPPY BELL CURVE

Current research on race and achievement is duping Black progressives and liberals into accepting Black inferiority.

STORY OF MY LIFE

I reprinted the following from one of my Facebook posts:

White researcher: "An African American child with a father who dropped out of high school has more than a 50 percent chance of seeing that father incarcerated by the time the child reaches age fourteen."

Black blogger: "The study shows that by the time a Black child turns 14, they are at 50 percent chance of seeing their father end up in prison."

Commenter 1: Single parents, culture of violence, Black people don't read ... Black people are trifling!

Commenter 2: Mass incarceration, school-to-prison pipeline ... Society is trifling!

Black Activist: "50 percent of Black kids gotta daddy in jail! If that's not a wakeup call, you ain't sleep, you in a coma!"

Black audience: [Cheers]

The Ambivalent: Hmmmmmmm?

Ivory Toldson: Many people are forwarding a recent article by The Grio that states, "The study shows that by the time a Black child turns 14, they are at 50 percent chance of seeing their father end up in prison." The study actually says, "An African American child with a father who dropped out of high school has more than a 50 percent chance of seeing that father incarcerated by the time the child reaches age fourteen." According to the NCES the "status dropout rate" for Black males was less than 10 percent in 2012. Therefore, across all Black males, take 10 percent and then take half of that, to determine the likelihood of a

© KONINKLIJKE BRILL NV, LEIDEN, 2019 | DOI:10.1163/9789004397040_002

child's father being incarcerated across the board. The Griot, I'm not trying to offend. I like the way you have represented my work in the past, and I appreciate what you are trying to do for the Black community. But please don't spread BS (Bad Stats).

Black audience: Hmmmmmmm?

Commenter 1: He's in denial.

Commenter 2: He's in denial.

Commenter 3: A White researcher at a prestigious institution conducted the original study. Dr. Toldson is not only Black, but he spent his entire academic career at an HBCU! I rest my case.

The Ambivalent: Thanks Dr. Toldson.

The Lesson: The Black community needs the ambivalent. We do not need the researcher, the blogger, the commenter, or the activist. We don't need anyone who thinks they have all the answers. We need people who are continually searching for the truth.

Black people need Black people who believe in Black people enough not to believe every bad thing they hear about Black people.

BS FUNNY NUMBERS

According to the U.S. Census, since 1970 there are 3.9 million less White males and 2.5 million more Black males, ages 15 to 25, in the U.S. population. So why do we often hear phrases like, "The reality is African-American males are a dying breed." Note the unqualified use of the word "reality." Also, note that "breed," "extinct" and "endangered" are terms reserved only for animals and Black males.

Dating back to the 1980s, before social media, people have applied these terms to Black men in peculiar ways – usually sensational and hyperbolic, but also casual and glib. Intended to sound an alarm, these phrases unwittingly normalized the murder of Black men like genocidal leaders who dehumanize their targets by likening their existence to animals.

The "dying breed" reference was quoted from an article called, "Report: 4 percent of college students are Black males" (Baber, 2012). The article features the laudable quest of Utica College to recruit more minority and low-income students. In an apparent attempt to draw readers in, the article adapted its title from a 2010 Council of the Great City Schools (CGCS) report, which found that "only 4 percent of college students are Black males" (Lewis, Simon, Uzzell, Horwitz, & Casserly, 2010). Although this figure has little to do with the actual article, it is an indisputable fact, right?

Let us examine the numbers. Today the 12.7 million Black males, who are 18 years old and older, comprise 5.5 percent of the adult population in the U.S. and the 76.4 million White males comprise 32.7 percent. According to the 2010 Census, the 1.2 million Black male college students comprised 5.5 percent of all college students, while the 5.6 million White male students comprised "just" 27 percent (Ruggles et al., 2015).

Similarly, I wrote a response to Trip Gabriel's New York Times editorial, "Proficiency of Black Students Is Found to Be Far Lower Than Expected" (Gabriel, 2010). Among my criticisms was that the author cited that Black males' representation in college of 5 percent was an indicator of failure. In a November 12th correction, Mr. Trip omitted that reference, noting "that figure did not represent one of the areas in which Blacks showed a lack of achievement." However, the spirit of the editorial remained unchanged, and unfortunately, reflects a larger problem of deficit statistics being promoted and embraced among people who would have challenged its merits years ago.

Notwithstanding, the situation for Black males in the United States is tenuous. Although 45 percent of Black males attempt college, only 16 percent have a four-year degree, half the percent of White males who have a four-year degree (Esters & Toldson, 2013). Black males are incarcerated at a rate that is seven times the rate for White males (Beck, 2000; West, 2010), and are more likely than any other race group to be a victim of a violent crime, including homicide.

Black people need not be insulated to their harsh realities, but much of the reported figures and statistics about Black people are poorly sourced, outdated, out of context, and not factual. For instance, the first paragraph of Russell Simmons' Huffington Post article, "Black Male Multiple Choice: Unemployed, High School Dropout or Incarcerated" is replete with factual errors.

Here, Simmons writes, "Black men represent 8 percent of the population of the United States but comprise 3 percent of all college undergrads." Does this sound familiar? In total, the first paragraph weaves about ten rogue statistics that together make Black men and boys seem hopeless and beyond repair. This is what Russell Simmons states:

> If a Black boy is born in the US today, he will have a 33 percent (FALSE) chance of going to prison in his lifetime. It has become a sad

normality, almost a backward rite of passage, for Black young men to enter the penal system (MYTH). Black men represent 8 percent (FALSE) of the population of the United States but comprise 3 percent (FALSE) of all college undergrads, 48 percent of inmates in prison (TRUE) and are five times more likely to die from HIV/AIDS than White men (OUT OF CONTEXT). Fifty percent of Black boys do not finish high school (FALSE), 72 percent of Black male dropouts in their 20s are unemployed, and 60 percent of Black male dropouts are eventually incarcerated (FALSE IF YOU BELIEVE THE 50% FIGURE).

Question: Dr. Toldson, so many people say, "1 in 3 Black men will serve time in prison in his lifetime," so why do you call it a lie or BS (bad stats)?

Answer: People say it because in 2003 a Bureau of Justice statistician named Thomas P. Bonczar (2003) published a report that stated: "About 1 in 3 Black males, 1 in 6 Hispanic males, and 1 in 17 White males are expected to go to prison during their lifetime, if current incarceration rates remain unchanged."

In a table called a "double decrement life table," Bonczar predicted the likelihood that a person would be incarcerated based on their race, gender and year of birth. The style of the study was very similar to John DiLulio's discredited "super-predator" research (more on that later).

The table header read "Percent ever going to prison during lifetime, born in ____." According to Bonczar, if you were a Black man born in 1974 (closer to my age) the likelihood was 13.4%, 1991 was 29.4%, and 2001 was 32.2% (1 in 3).

Importantly, the report was published in 2003, so the 1 in 3 was only applicable to 2-year-olds. The rate given for Black men generally at the time was 22%, but even that figure is a bit suspect (as it was merely the cumulative prediction, not the actual rate).

About a decade and a half later, we still quote this 1 in 3 stat (usually without citing). Notwithstanding, those 2-year-olds, now at the brink of adulthood, can proudly proclaim to be the least violent generation of Black people in modern history.

As a member of the generation that invented drive-bys, Jordan-jacking, Crips and Bloods, gangsta rap, and discharging guns at the movies, I'd like to thank today's Black teenagers for being so much better than the 1980s-90s version of my indignant-as-adult Black peers.

THE HAPPY BELL CURVE

In 1994, when Harvard psychologist Richard J. Herrnstein and American Enterprise Institute political scientist Charles Murray released "The Bell Curve" (Herrnstein & Murray, 1994), the book immediately drew fiery rebuttals from progressive scholars. Featured articles in the *Journal of Negro Education* (Graves Jr, 1995; Madhere, 1995) and the *Journal of Black Psychology* (Price & Cutler, 2001) were devoted to picking apart, point-by-point, such dangerous assertions as, "It seems highly likely to us that both genes and the environment have something to do with racial differences [in intelligence and by extension achievement]."

Table 2.1. The bell curve

Bell curve	Happy bell curve

Conservative, liberal, and progressive academics use similar, inherently racist, instruments to assert or acquiesce to Black inferiority.

"A Call for Change: The Social and Educational Factors Contributing to the Outcomes of Black Males in Urban Schools" made the bogus assertions that racial differences cannot be explained by economic factors and that Black males without disabilities do not measure up to White males with disabilities (Lewis et al., 2010).

The report quite pointedly stated, "Black males without disabilities had reading and mathematics scores, on average, lower than those of White males in national public schools with disabilities," and made similar comparisons using those who do and do not receive free and reduced lunch (Lewis et al., 2010). Unlike 1994, Black progressives mostly embraced the work of the CGCS, giving them endless platforms to explain how our normal Black boys are more academically inept than are White boys with disabilities.

The fact that Black students receive lower scores on standardized tests has been documented in more than a half century of research studies. What is less well documented is the predictive validity of these tests. The SAT and GRE for example, do a much poorer job predicting college or grad school success than grade point average. In addition, with both tests, very high scores are much better predictors of future success, than very low scores are predictors of future failure.

Due to the established unresolved issues with cultural bias in all achievement tests, "The Standards for Educational and Psychological Testing" recommends using the norms for specific race groups as a basis of making decisions. In addition, test scores should always be presented as an estimate with the margin of error revealed and disclaimers indicating that issues of cultural bias limit the degree of confidence one should place in assessment results. This is consistent with prudent testing practices as developed by the *American Educational Research Association, American Psychological Association*, and the *National Council on Measurement in Education*.

On the issue of students with disabilities, the report refers to Black and White students with and without "disabilities," about 50 times, but never defines specific disabilities to which they are referring. With the vast range of disabilities affecting children, it seems inappropriate to lump them all in the same category. Oddly after doing a document search of common adjectives that typically precede "disabilities," words including "emotional," "physical," and "learning" did not appear anywhere in the report. Before accepting, at face value, that normal Black boys are less proficient than disabled White boys, at minimum one should seek a definition of disability. Many students, who receive a proper diagnosis of a learning disability, also receive educational accommodations, especially during testing, that could improve performance.

Overall, it seems the bell curve has been flipped upside down, and now appears more as a smile than a scowl. But the message is the same, no matter how it is packaged. Implicit in the findings of *The Bell Curve, A Call for Change*, and the countless reports and articles about Black male failure, is the notion that underachievement among Black people is so elusive and refractory to change, that it must be a relatively stable fixture in the disposition of the Black community.

Culturally biased assessment practices and institutional racism continue to be at the core of the impending "national catastrophe" so glibly forewarned by "A Call for Change." Incidentally, in the 120-page report, the words "cultural," "racism" and "bias" do not appear once; not even as a remote possibility for the racial differences they found.

The authors also manage to report low achievement indicators for White males but allow them to shine next to the absurdly low numbers for Black males. For example, it is surprising that only 38 percent of White boys were proficient in reading, with the social advantages afforded to them. Yet even more vexing is how this society can establish a metric that only finds 25 percent of Black and White boys combined proficient in reading and consider it valid.

In general, the nation's response to educational disparities is reminiscent of how we responded to AIDS in the 1980s. By designating AIDS as a gay disease, proactive solutions were stalled by moral invectives and political twaddle. Similarly, when you really dig into the numbers, educational inferiority is less of a Black male problem and more of an American problem. If trends continue, educational disparities between Black and White will pale in comparison to American education and educational systems in other developed nations.

Scholars, activists, and policymakers should pause and contemplate the benefits and risks of promoting negative racial deficit statistics. What have we gained in the past and what do we stand to gain in the future? In the previous chapter, I suggested that educational researchers should reduce the focus on comparing Black males to White males. This lazy research method implicitly positions White male standings as the standard for Black males to achieve. Instead, we should compare Black males with high levels of proficiency in reading and mathematics to those with lower levels. This is the only method that will reveal culturally specific strategies to improve educational standings among Black males.

Concerns regarding Black males in education are real and pervasive, but we do not need to harvest negative propaganda to promote change. Overstated and unqualified deficit statistics have the consequence of falsely promoting Black inferiority. Whether upside down or right side up, skewed left or skewed right, *The Bell Curve* remains an invertible force that undermines Black achievement, by using numbers to obscure legitimate indicators such as graduation rates, college enrollment, and economic attainment, while neglecting social forces such as social inequities and institutional racism.

WHY NOT TRUST OBJECTIVE RESEARCH ON BLACK PEOPLE?

'Objectivity' was adopted as a standard in research at a time when the academy was dominated by White men who wanted everyone to believe that: (1) They knew more about oppressed people than oppressed people knew about themselves; and (2) Being a survivor of oppression limits, rather than enhances, your ability to be a good researcher.

Researchers inherently look for problems among Black people. Therefore, most "objective" research studies conclude that Black folks are 'messed up.' For example, as a young professor at Howard University, I participated in a workshop at the University of Michigan to learn how to conduct multivariate analyses of the U.S. Census using IPUMS files. A White professor from Georgia State University assisted with the training.

After I conducted a simple analysis comparing the Black population to the White population on a social characteristic, I did not find a significant difference. As I studied the findings, the White professor leaned over my shoulder and said,

"I bet if you ran the analysis 'this' way, instead of 'that' way, you'd find what you're looking for."

My response was, "How do you know what I'm looking for?"

"So, if a researcher finds something right about Black people, the research must be wrong?" We must read studies about Black people with caution. Most of them are BS.

W.E.B. Du Bois said, "One could not be a calm, cool, and detached scientist while Negroes are lynched, murdered, and starved."

It reminded me of my first year as a professor. "Needlessly contentious and emotionally loaded" was in the written feedback of a rejection letter that I received from a top tier peer-refereed academic journal. The rejection letter was for an article that I wrote about Black men in the criminal justice system. If you're a scholar doing work for the betterment of Black people, and no one has ever called you something like contentious, emotional, angry, subjective, or impatient, you're probably not doing much.

The following are some of my unapologetic rantings as a needlessly wilfully contentious and emotionally loaded scholar:

My Social Media Response to New York Times, "1.5 Million Missing Black Men"

In 2015, Three White men named Justin Wolfers, David Leonhardt and Kevin Quealy authored a story for the New York Times reporting that 1.5 Million Black men are "missing" from the U.S. population.

They used publicly available census data and a simplistic analysis (essentially looking at the proportion of Black men to Black women by city). Since any graduate student could conduct the analysis, one could only assume that NYT thought so little of Black people that they believed they needed White men to provide the proper context to OUR situation, or to give the article credibility.

Black people hear this: Our sons are dying and being imprisoned by a racially biased criminal justice system. We don't need the glib analysis of a White-privileged team of researchers, who have made us unwitting research subjects, to reinforce our pain. We need our personal observations and experiences, and the good research of good people who actually work with our community. We don't need the BS (bad stats) of people who evade the peer-review process and create sensational sound bites and charts from census data.

The other side of the story: According to the U.S. Census, there are more Black men in the U.S. population today than at any other point in history. Since 1990, Black men have gained nearly 1 million people in our most vulnerable age group (15–25). By contrast, White men have LOST almost 700,000 from the same age group. The NYT lumped our brothers who die of heart disease after the age of 50, with our brothers who missed the census due to incarceration to create a compounding effect. Fact: The noninstitutionalized population of the U.S. has been consistently making steady gains among Black men and steady losses among White men for nearly 40 years. No analysis can dispute this.

Black people need strength and conviction, not media generated consternation.

We need tireless advocates, not cultural voyeurs, and opportunists.

We need good research on SPECIFIC issues that plague our community, not broad brush BS.

My Social Media Response to New York Times "Extensive Data Shows Punishing Reach of Racism for Black Boys"

The NYT article about Rich Black families raising poor Black men is trash. It's written from the garbage White liberal perspective that Black people need to back away from. It alludes to cultural deficits in the Black community, and micro-level racial biases, and ignores the larger systemic forces that are directly accountable for their findings.

25

They used the 2010 census for this study, only two years after the recession and mortgage crisis. However, they failed to mention old White money that preyed on new Black money, unregulated banks that gave subprime loans, and the sharks who took out insurance and made money when Black people defaulted on loans.

The article attempts to blame to blame things like incarceration and marriage, based on the weakest links to their study. At the same time, they ignore basic flaws in our economy, the corporate welfare, that makes old money make money without trying, and new money vulnerable to capitalist greed.

They said, "The sons of Black families from the top 1 percent had about the same chance of being incarcerated on a given day as the sons of White families earning $36,000." That sounds bad, until you look at the graph closer, and realize that the actual incarceration rate for children of the top Black income earners is 2%. And that isn't the bottom for all Black people. Black people in the top 5% had children with a lower incarceration rate than those in the top 1%. This has NOTHING to do with Black people's inability to transfer wealth intergenerationally.

They said, "There's a large gap in the marriage rates of White and Black Americans, even after accounting for income." On this graph, they only look at adults age 32–37. Why only this age? What is the point of excluding people who got married at < 31 or > 38? Again, this has NOTHING to do with Black people's inability to transfer wealth intergenerationally.

The average White 1 percenter inherited $4 million. White wealth is different from Black wealth because the system is rigged. We should NOT discuss why Black people don't have enough money; we should discuss why White MEN have so much of it. In public, rich White men talk about hard work; privately, they talk about passive income and beating the system by hedging, rather than working hard.

Stay away from NYT's continuous disingenuous analyses of Black issues. Let's stop inhaling liberal farts. We need a thoughtful analysis of White people and White wealth.

Show us how to golf all day and still be rich.

Show us how to make money while other people, especially Black people, lose money.

Show us how to have less education than Asians but still make more money than them.

Show us how to file for bankruptcy and default on loans and still be rich.

NYT, until you do, I'll show you the recycle bin.

My Response to "Demographic Patterns of Cumulative Arrest Prevalence by Ages 18 and 23" Published in Crime & Delinquency

This week, countless media outlets bemoaned a study's findings that suggested that 49% of Black males and 38% of White males have been arrested by the time they turn 23. If you are the parent of a Black male, they suggest that the hue of your son's skin could make his likelihood of being arrested akin to a coin toss. Parents of White males should also be worried that nearly 40 percent of their son's peers will be marred by a criminal record, but at least they can take solace in the fact that their sons fair better than Black males.

Robert Brame, Shawn D. Bushway, Ray Paternoster, and Michael G. Turner published the study in *Crime & Delinquency*. The study is so replete with error that it should never have been released for public discourse. If you read the article, you will find that it is more of an experiment on handling missing waves of data from a longitudinal sample than a meaningful study about race, gender, and crime.

In the method section, they devote more than a page on their strategy for handling missing data. On how they measured arrests, they write "Based on survey questions about arrest experiences, we compiled historical information about arrest experiences through ages 18 and 23 for each person" and nothing else. They don't list the survey questions in an appendix nor discuss the reliability or validity of the items. Without this basic information, the study cannot be replicated, which disqualifies it from being considered good science.

However, the biggest flaw is that the study's sample of Non-Hispanic Black males was only 537 who fully participated and 58 who were "missing at random." Those who were "missing at random" participated in the first round of interviews in the longitudinal study but provided insufficient information in subsequent interviews. In the study methods, someone who had not been arrested at the time of the first interview could be assigned an arrest based on the patterns of their peers. Thus, Black males could be guilty by association even in a dataset.

The data the authors used was self-report data from the U.S. Department of Labor's National Longitudinal Survey of Youth, 1997 cohort (NLYS97). The arrest data in the NLYS97 are meant to be supplemental. The NLSY97 youths were 12 to 16 years old as of December 31, 1996 and were interviewed between 1997 and 2008. The respondents are 29 to 34 years old now. According to the Office of Juvenile Justice and Delinquency Prevention the overall arrest rate for Black juveniles peaked in 1995. Between their peak year and 2010, the juvenile arrest rates declined by 40% for Black juveniles. Therefore, the study really examines a reflection and the immediate aftermath of the peak in juvenile arrests, almost two decades later.

Although the study is new, the data is old. The study also contributes nothing new to our collective understanding about race and the law. The study used self-report data on a group of Black males that would not quite fill a gymnasium, when direct data from court records are available. We have legitimate issues related to sentencing disparities and school-based arrest, but this study and the ensuing articles are nothing more than stunts designed to create sound bites for culture critics, caricatures of young Black men, and fodder for popular discourse (or righteous indignation).

The research team has no ethnic or gender diversity, yet they attempt to address complex relationships between race, gender, and likelihood of being arrested during childhood and young adulthood. The study, "Demographic Patterns of Cumulative Arrest Prevalence by Ages 18 and 23," handles provocative findings in a manner that is glib and disconnected, and rehashes trite themes without offering any meaningful solutions. Of the findings, the authors suggest, "Future research should focus on the identification and management of collateral risks that often accompany arrest experiences." If they consider this "future research" they are dreadfully late to the conversation.

Letter to the Author of "Demographic Patterns of Cumulative Arrest Prevalence by Ages 18 and 23"

Dr. Brame,

As you write about race and arrests, please take great care to protect the integrity of your research, because millions of young Black men suffer the consequences of the negative perceptions and stereotype threat associated with grim statistics. Although your study is deeply flawed, it has gained considerable media attention and will undoubtedly shape attitudes about young Black men and boys in an educational system that is already hypervigilant in their management of security and discipline.

Below is a link to the article that I wrote about your study. I have already shared this information with the editor of Crime & Delinquency in hopes that you both will adhere to higher standards of scholarship in future research in this area. I also suggest that you diversify your research team when researching issues of race and gender, so that you understand how to present your findings in a manner that respects the communities that have unwittingly become your subject.

Best,

Ivory

To White People Who Conduct Research on Black People

I once met a young White woman who told me that her major area of research was Black males. I immediately responded, "My major area of research is White women." She started blushing, but I retorted in all seriousness and asked, "What would you think if you met a Black man who was researching White women?" She admitted that she'd be suspicious. I don't blame her. There's no obvious connection, however, some have deemed me racist for questioning the motives of White people who study Black issues.

White people who objectively studied Black issues reported that slaves who wanted to escape had "drapetomania" (Goodheart, 2015), warned of "cocaine-crazed Negros" (Des Jarlais, 2015), unethically refused treatment to Black men with syphilis (Warren, Williams, & Wilson, 2012), biased the nation against single Black mothers (PR Newswire, 2015), reported that Black children born to crack addicts would grow up to damage society, reported "Black children born in the early 1990s would become super-predators" (DiLulio, 1995), and falsely reported that there were more Black men in prison than in college (Ziedenberg & Schiraldi, 2002). Black people would be foolish not to be suspicious of White researchers.

However, I know White people who do good research on Black people. Good White researchers on Black issues:

- Understand their subjective limitations and work with Black people to better inform their research;
- Understand the role of White privilege in their own success, and work to make sure that the community they research tangibly benefit from their studies;
- Conduct research on Black 'humans' and strive to have a deeper understanding of the Black experience, rather than studying the Black "population";
- Never cast a spotlight on Black problems without highlighting the important work germinating from within the Black community; and
- Do not see themselves as saviors, but as allies.

Usually, White people who research Black people have more to gain from the research than Black people – It is up to us to change this.

But before we change this, Black people need people who believe in Black people enough not to believe every bad thing they hear about Black people.

Silence the White researchers who objectify and exploit Black people and uplift the true allies.

Lifting the Cloak of White Objectivity to Reveal a Powerful Black Nation Hidden in Plain Sight

Ahead of its nationwide release, I, along with my wife and daughter, attended a pre-screening of the *Black Panther*, in the Oprah Winfrey Theatre at The Smithsonian National Museum of African American History and Culture (NMAAHC). The event featured a panel discussion with the *Black Panther* director, Ryan Coogler, and costume designer Ruth E. Carter. The regal Black museum, with a theatre named after a Black woman billionaire, hosting a talented Black director and designer, showing a movie featuring a Black cast in an intrepid Black nation was spectacular.

The image of Black excellence displayed at the *Black Panther* screening contradicted the reality of many Black people. Weeks after the screening, a new study, "Healing Our Divided Society: Investing in America Fifty Years After the Kerner Report," revealed that African Americans have made no progress in homeownership, employment, and incarceration in 50 years (Harris & Curtis, 2018).

The original Kerner Commission report was published in 1968, two years after the Black Panther was originally conceived. Marvel Comics created the Black Panther in 1966 (Gray, 2016), a few months before the Black Panther Party started in Oakland, California and at the tipping point of racial divisions that led to hundreds of race riots across the United States (Editorial Staff, 2016).

The Black Panther series featured a Black man as one of Marvel's strongest and most intelligent superheroes, fighting against the Ku Klux Klan in 1976 and confronting South African apartheid authorities in 1989. Yet, in the decades since the Black Panther's debut, numerous indicators continue to show that Black people are not making social progress. Today, as we reconcile the *Black Panther* movie's audacious display of Black genius with the glooming narrative of "Healing Our Divided Society," many conclude that Black progress is merely fiction.

Despite immeasurable odds against us, Black people have made remarkable progress in the United States, and any lack of progress is due to White supremacy and systemic racism, not cultural ineptitude. White men using "objective" research have led to most, if not all, of the reports that have obfuscated Black progress, including the Kerner Report.

The Kerner Report used a cloak of objectivity to measure Black social progress against White social standards. Notwithstanding many useful research methods and strategies derived from objective research, objectivity as an exclusive research paradigm is vulnerable to error and prejudice.

Black Americans are more like the fictional nation of Wakanda than they are like their disingenuous portrayals in classic objective research. The world viewed Wakanda as a third world country with limited technological abilities, yet they hid their genius in plain sight. African Americans are similar. In many ways, we have used negative perceptions to our advantage.

African Americans survived the transatlantic slave trade, maroon colony massacres, reconstruction betrayal, lynching, race riots that targeted Black enterprise, Jim Crow laws, COINTELPRO, the U.S.-Contra crack imports, the prison industrial complex, and a wave of murders of unarmed Black civilians.

Yet, through centuries of state sponsored terror against Black Americans, we continue to achieve and progress. *NPR* reported that Black youth use computer technology more than any other race (Westervelt, 2016). *The Washington Post* reported that the Black incarceration rate is declining faster than that of any other race (Humphreys, 2016). There are 2 million more Black people in college today than twenty years ago (Toldson & Morton, 2011), and Black people continue to make advances in every field of human endeavor.

Black social, political, and economic gains have been ubiquitous for more than a century. Morgan State University professor, Stacey Patton, aptly proclaimed:

Before the fictitious Wakanda there was: Atlanta before 1906, Tulsa's 'Black Wall Street,' East St. Louis before 1917, Chicago before 1919, Washington, DC before 1919, Knoxville, TN before 1919, and Rosewood. These are examples of just seven thriving, self-sufficient, successful Black communities before they were destroyed by White supremacist violence. (Patton, 2018)

The key difference, however, between Wakandans and African Americans, is that Wakandans never believed or internalized the false perceptions that other nations had of them. When African Americans stop believing negative statistics derived from objectivist research, and start believing in ourselves, we can be a nation as strong as Wakanda.

REFERENCES

Baber, C. (2012, February 18). Report: 4 percent of college students are Black males. *Observer-Dispatch*. Retrieved from https://www.uticaod.com/article/20120218/NEWS/302189964

Beck, A. J. (2000). *Prison and jail inmates at midyear 1999* (NCJ Publication No. 181643). Washington, DC: U.S. Department of Justice.

Bonczar, T. P. (2003). *Bureau of justice statistics special report: Prevalence of imprisonment in the U.S. population, 1974–2001*. Washington, DC. Retrieved from https://www.bjs.gov/content/pub/pdf/piusp01.pdf

Des Jarlais, D. C. (2015). The fear of drugs used by strangers. *Substance Use & Misuse, 50*(8–9), 987–989. doi:10.3109/10826084.2015.1015354

DiLulio, J. (1995). The coming of the super-predators. *The Weekly Standard*. Retrieved from https://www.weeklystandard.com/john-j-dilulio-jr/the-coming-of-the-super-predators

Editorial Staff. (2016). 50 years of the Black panther party. *Ebony, 71*(10), 102.

Esters, L. L., & Toldson, I. A. (2013). Supporting minority male education in Science, Technology, Engineering, and Mathematics (STEM) disciplines. *Texas Education Review, 1*, 209–219.

Gabriel, T. (2010, November 10). Proficiency of Black students is found to be far lower than expected. *New York Times*, p. A22. Retrieved from https://www.nytimes.com/2010/11/09/education/09gap.html

Goodheart, A. (2015). The secret history of the underground railroad. *Atlantic, 315*(2), 48–50.

Graves Jr, J. L. (1995). The pseudoscience of psychometry and the bell curve. *Journal of Negro Education, 64*(3), 277.

Gray, J. W. (2016). Son of the Black panther. *New Republic, 247*(6), 76–79.

Harris, F., & Curtis, A. (2018). *Healing our divided society: Investing in America fifty years after the Kerner report Hardcove*. Philadelphia, PA: Temple University Press.

Herrnstein, R. J., & Murray, C. A. (1994). *The bell curve: Intelligence and class structure in American life*. New York, NY: Free Press.

Humphreys, K. (2016). There's been a big decline in the black incarceration rate, and almost nobody's paying attention. *The Washington Post*. Retrieved from https://www.washingtonpost.com/news/wonk/wp/2016/02/10/almost-nobody-is-paying-attention-to-this-massive-change-in-criminal-justice/?utm_term=.c150a752900e

Lewis, S., Simon, C., Uzzell, R., Horwitz, A., & Casserly, M. (2010). *A call for change: The social and educational factors contributing to the outcomes of Black males in urban schools*. Washington, DC: The Council of the Great City Schools. Retrieved from http://www.edweek.org/media/black_male_study.pdf

Madhere, S. (1995). Beyond the bell curve: Toward a model of talent and character development. *Journal of Negro Education, 64*(3), 326.

Patton, S. (2018). [Response to the Black Panther].

Price, J. D., & Cutler, C. E. (2001). Games intellectuals play: Authority, power, and intelligence. *Journal of Black Psychology, 27*(4), 477–495. doi:10.1177/0095798401027004006

PR Newswire. (2015). The Moynihan report at 50: New report finds that the rise of single mothers does not explain poverty rates fully. *IWPR-Moynihan-Report*.

Ruggles, S., Sobek, M., Alexander, T., Fitch, C. A., Goeken, R., Hall, P. K., … Ronnander, C. (2015). *Integrated public use microdata series: Version 4.0* [Machine-readable database]. Minneapolis, MN: Minnesota Population Center.

Toldson, I. A., & Morton, J. (2011). Editor's comment: A million reasons there're more Black men in college than in prison; Eight hundred thousand reasons there's more work to be done. *Journal of Negro Education, 80*(1), 1–4.

Warren, R. C., Williams, L. S., & Wilson, W. D. (2012). Addressing the legacy of the U.S. public health service syphilis study at Tuskegee: Optimal health in health care reform philosophy. *Ethics and Behavior, 22*(6), 496–500.

West, H. C. (2010). *Prison inmates at Midyear 2009 – Statistical tables*. Washington, DC: Bureau of Justice Statistics. Retrieved from http://www.bjs.gov/content/pub/pdf/pim09st.pdf

Westervelt, E. (2016). Being Black in the tech industry. *NPR.com*. Retrieved from https://www.npr.org/2016/02/28/468483901/being-black-in-the-tech-industry

Ziedenberg, J., & Schiraldi, V. (2002). *Cellblocks or classrooms? The funding of higher education and corrections and its impact on African American men*. Retrieved from http://www.justicepolicy.org/research/2046Schoorman

MORE BLACK MEN IN PRISON THAN COLLEGE

Why the line, "More Black Men in Prison than College" is the mother of all BS.

***

What does the line, "There are more Black men in jail than in college" have in common with the Jheri Curl? ANSWER: They were invented by White men (Vincent Schiraldi and Jheri Redding, respectively), worn badly by Black people, and left a nasty stain on the shoulders of millions of Black men.

It's been more than 20 years since the Jheri Curl faded away into infamy, and I'm proud to say that even in the 1980s, I never sported a curl. Unfortunately, I can't say the same about the line, "There are more Black men in jail than in college."

About five years ago I wrote, "In 2000, the Justice Policy Institute (JPI) found evidence that more Black men are in prison than in college," in my first *Breaking Barriers* report (Toldson, 2008). At the time, I did not question the veracity of this statement. The statement fit well among other stats that I used to establish the need for more solution-focused research on Black male achievement.

I was in good company. The same year, at a 2007 NAACP forum, then Presidential Candidate Obama said, "We have more work to do when more young Black men languish in prison than attend colleges and universities across America" (Kesssler, 2007).

Both President Obama and I brought our own unique style to the line. I was deferential and academic, while President Obama was passionate and eloquent. In contrast, many people like Charles Barkley, are reckless and aloof when they use the line. He said, "You know, we as Black people always, we don't have respect for one another. You know, we've got more Black men in prison than we do in college and crime in our neighborhoods is running rampant" (Howerton, 2012). In full context, Charles Barkley was using the line to justify the need for armed defense against Black men to Bob Costas.

© KONINKLIJKE BRILL NV, LEIDEN, 2019 | DOI:10.1163/9789004397040_003

However, just as a Jheri Curl would be wrong no matter how you dressed it up today, the line, "There are more Black men in jail than in college," is wrong no matter how you contextualize, qualify, or articulate it. Today, there are approximately six hundred thousand more Black men in college than jail, and the best research evidence suggests that the line was never true. In this chapter, I examine the dubious origins, widespread use, and harmful effects of what is arguably the most frequently quoted statistic about Black men in the United States.

THE DUBIOUS BASIS FOR THE LINE, "THERE ARE MORE BLACK MEN IN JAIL THAN IN COLLEGE"

More than 10 years ago, JPI released the report "Cellblocks or Classrooms" (Ziedenberg & Schiraldi, 2002). The report admonished federal and state governments for abdicating their role of providing equitable social resources and access to higher education, while building a colossal prison system, largely on the backs of nonviolent drug offenders. While the report should have been a wakeup call to policymakers, one line resonated and echoed more than any other: "Nearly a third more African American men are incarcerated than in higher education."

JPI has yet to acknowledge that the enrollment of Black males in college is drastically different today, from when they published *Cellblocks or Classrooms*. If we replicated JPI's analysis by downloading enrollment data from the National Center for Education Statistics' Integrated Post-Secondary Education Data System (IPEDS), we would find a 108.5% jump in Black male college enrollment from 2001 to 2011 (Knapp, Kelly-Reid, & Ginder, 2010). In raw numbers the enrollment of Black males increased from 693,044 in 2001 to 1,445,194 in 2011 (U.S. Department of Education's National Center for Education Statistics, 2012).

In September 2012, in response to the Congressional Black Caucus Foundation's screening of the film Hoodwinked, directed by Janks Morton, JPI issued a press release titled, "JPI Stands by Data in 2002 on Education and Incarceration" (Justice Policy Institute, 2012). However, when examining the data from 2001 to 2011, many colleges and universities were not reporting their data ten years ago.

In 2011, 4,503 colleges and universities across the United States reported having at least one Black male student (U.S. Department of Education's National Center for Education Statistics, 2012). In 2001, only 2,734 colleges and universities reported having at least one Black male student, with more than one thousand not reporting any data at all. When perusing through the list of colleges with significant Black male populations today, but reported none in 2001, I noticed several historically Black colleges and universities, including Bowie State University, and my own alma mater, Temple University. Ironically, I was enrolled at Temple as a doctoral candidate in 2001. Therefore, it seems that I, along with hundreds of thousands of other Black male college students, were not counted when JPI estimated that there were more Black men in prison than in college.

IPEDS seems to improve every year and more recent data has much better cross validity with data from the American Community Survey (ACS). IPEDS receives data from colleges and universities, and the ACS receives data from the students. Remarkably, in 2010 IPEDS recorded 1,391,500 (Ruggles et al., 2009), and the ACS recorded 1,391,510 Black male college students – a difference of only 10 students. This is in stark contrast to the year 2000 when the difference between the two reporting agencies was 373,400 students. See the image, "Black Male College Enrollment and Incarceration from 2001–2011," for more details.

I do not believe JPI initially attempted to mislead the public. As a researcher who uses large datasets, I understand the inherent margin of error associated with such analysis. However, I do think they show arrogance and imprudence when they "stand by" their original findings today. The increase in Black male college enrollment over the last ten years is due to three primary factors: (1) IPEDS more precisely tracking enrollment (artificial gains); (2) social advancements (authentic gains); and (3) the rise of community and for-profit colleges (authentic gains).

Persistence of the Myth against the Changing Landscape for Black Men in Higher Education

Black male on Twitter: Son, there are more Black men in Trenton State Prison than in every college in NJ [New Jersey]. This is a sad fact of the struggle @toldson is wrong.

@toldson: NJ has 63 colleges that enroll 25,473 total Black males. Essex CC [Community College] has most. The total (all race) prison population in NJ is 24,590.

Black male on Twitter: @toldson I suppose if we count 2-year institutes perhaps the numbers get better, but when I attend a class at Rutgers with 275, no way I should be of one.

> @*toldson*: This is the way. Rutgers has a student body of 52,471 and only 1,261 Black males. My numbers aren't always pretty, but they're real.

Technology, costs, demographic shifts, and emerging occupational requirements are creating fundamental changes in the higher education landscape. Today, distance learning, community colleges, and for-profit colleges are offering Black students cost- and time-efficient alternatives to traditional colleges, yet many questions remain about the quality of education they provide. In 2001, four HBCUs were among the top ten for enrolling Black males. In 2011, no HBCUs were in the top ten and only one (Florida A&M University) was in the top twenty. The top ten colleges for enrolling Black males are comprised of three for-profit colleges, four community colleges, and three public 4-year institutions. University of Phoenix – Online Campus reported 847 Black male students in 2001 and 21,802 in 2011, making it the nation's top enroller of Black male students. Second to the top is Ashford University, which reported 23 Black males in 2001 and 15,081 in 2011 (U.S. Department of Education's National Center for Education Statistics, 2012).

Importantly, Black males' representation in higher education is proportional to their representation in the adult population. However, lack of adequate advisement and academic rigor in high schools has resulted in Black males being underrepresented at competitive universities like Rutgers and overrepresented at community colleges and online universities. Consider this: If all 1,127,170 Black males who were enrolled in undergraduate programs in 2010 eventually graduated, the total number of Black males with college degrees would increase by 71%, nearly achieving parity with White males. However, we will not sufficiently support Black male college students, nor college bound students, if we simply juxtapose their needs to Black males in the criminal justice system.

THE OVERREPRESENTATION OF BLACK MEN IN PRISON CONTINUES TO BE A PROBLEM

Trends over the last ten years have shown little evidence that the United States has resolved longstanding racial disparities in sentencing and incarcerating Black men (West, 2010). There are 49,400 more Black men in jail and prisons today than there were ten years ago; however, the rate of incarceration has not changed. In 2009, Black males represented 40 percent of the total male prison population, compared with 45 percent in 2000. In 2000, there were 4,777 Black men in jail for every 100,000 Black men in the U.S. population, compared to 4,749 Black men in prison in 2009. Although the rate increase among White males was higher during that time period (from 683 to 708), the current rate for Black males is still almost seven times that of White males.

Beyond the flaws in the numbers, *Cellblocks or Classrooms* argued for fair economic, educational, and criminal justice policies, as well as responsible allocation of public resources from state and federal governments. Recent evidence supports the premise that priorities to incarcerate compete against priorities to educate. Today, Louisiana, the state with the highest rate of incarceration among males (1,665), has the lowest percentage of Black males who have completed college (9 percent). Other states with low percentages of Black males who completed college (9–10 percent), including Mississippi, Arkansas, and South Carolina, also had incarceration rates well above the national average of 954. By contrast, Vermont, the state with the highest percentage of Black males with college degrees (46 percent), has an incarceration rate of 528 for males.

STARTING A NEW AGENDA TO INCREASE COLLEGE PERSISTENCE AND REDUCE INCARCERATION FOR BLACK MALES

"There're more Black men in jail than in college" is a line that has transfigured our understanding of persistent problems among Black men in the United States. Many activists and scholars recite it to invoke a level of urgency to fight unjust social structures, while culture critics say it to condemn the social failings of Black men. The line is memorable, immutable, provocative, and but, piercing unfortunately, it is not true. This reality does not necessarily call into question the credibility of thousands of well-intentioned programs and social activists; however, it does present an opportunity for Black Americans to realign our priorities and address new realities. The following are some unintended consequences of spreading this myth about Black men:

The Myth Leaves Young Black Men Vulnerable to Stereotypes

I remember showing, "Bring Your 'A' Game" to a group of Black male high school students in Harrisburg, PA. In the movie, narrator Mario Van Peebles emphatically states, "There are more Black men in prison than in college – That's a fact!" When the movie concluded I asked the young males to react to that specific line. Their response was sullen and disappointed. When I told them the real numbers, their mood immediately changed to hopeful and inspired.

A White female teacher from New York City further explained, "This has negative effects on both ends, as teachers formulate stereotypes about Black male students, and these students fight less to battle those stereotypes. The result is the academic failure of Black male students who feel as though the school system failed them long before they gave up on the system."

The Myth Causes Us to Set the Bar too Low and Establish Misguided Policies for Black Men

The idea that we are losing Black males in college to the criminal justice system distracts us from very real issues and leads to the erroneous conclusion that violence prevention and gang abatement programs will increase college enrolment among Black males. Merely achieving college enrollment that exceeds incarceration is not an acceptable objective. Black males need programs, like honors and AP classes, academic advisement, and academic clubs, to help them to excel in school and graduate from college. Also, as the current numbers suggest, we can have adequate representation in college, while at the same time have low graduation rates and extremely high incarceration rates. Therefore, we should separate prison reform efforts from college recruitment, retention and graduation efforts.

The Myth Focuses on Black Men and Not the System

To the average system loyalist, more Black men in prison than college, simply means Black men need to commit crime less and study in school more. Issues like sentencing disparities, income inequity, and institutional racism are not necessarily implied by the myth.

Recently, a new line started to emerge as a popular sound bite. The line "More Black men are in prison today than were enslaved in 1850" has become the favorite takeaway from a very remarkable book called *The New Jim Crow*, by Michelle Alexander. Alfred Edmond, Jr. explained the flaws with such a statement in his article for Black Enterprise, so I won't repeat them here. Instead, I'll offer a set of lines, from an article I wrote last year, that focus the problem away from Black men and onto the system:

> After the dust settled from the Iran-Contra scandal, the War on Drugs continued to function as the middle passage between poor Black neighborhoods and prison industries that thrived on cheap prison labor. Inmates with better health and lower security risk typically worked for a prison industry called UNICOR for about 23 cents per hour. From

this, one can surmise that a system that gives longer prison sentences to less violent offenders can generate a healthy profit. In 2008, UNICOR reported $854.3 million in sales, nearly twice their earnings of 1996.

No, this is not as easy to say or digest, but it is a more accurate depiction of the link between slavery and the prison industrial complex. I recommend reading *The New Jim Crow*, in its entirety to get a clearer perspective on the systemic challenges and policy solutions for mass-incarceration among Black males.

Conclusion, Context, Dissection and the Surge of White Women in Prison

According to the Department of Justice, between 2000 and 2009 the rate increase among White women in jails and prisons was greater than any other race-gender group (Beck, 2000). During the ten-year period, the rate of incarceration decreased for Black men by .6%, decreased for Black women by 12%, and *increased* for White women by 44%. In 2000, there were more Black women in prison than any other race of women. By 2009, at 92,100, the White female prison population was nearly as high as the Black female (64,800) and Hispanic female (32,300) prison population combined (97,100).

These are factual statements, but skeptics will point out that because of "regression toward the mean," percent changes are elusive when comparing the large starting point of Black male incarceration rate to the small starting point of the White female incarceration rate. However, a 44% rate increase is not a complete anomaly, and many who work within the prison system attribute the gains to the rise of crystal meth use among poor rural White women.

Dissecting and contextualizing stats pertaining to White people is natural. We should apply the same diligence when seeking to understand stats about Black people. The prison to college population comparison, from its onset, has been dubious because it essentially compares college life, a time and age-restricted experience, to prison life, a condition with an unlimited range of sentences and ages. The U.S. Census estimates that approximately 17,945,068 people in the U.S. population are Black males, irrespective of age. Among them, about 6.3 percent are in college and 4.7 percent are in prison. The remaining 89 percent have already graduated from college, already served a prison sentence, have a life trajectory that does not involve college or prison, or are too young for either to apply (Ruggles et al., 2009).

When reviewing *Cellblocks or Classrooms*, there's no evidence that the authors intended to sensationalize problems facing Black men in the United States. Today, the widespread and erroneous notion that "there are more Black men in jail than in college" is not the fault of JPI. Rather, it is the fault of journalists looking for a sound bite, politicians trying to arouse a crowd, program managers and researchers who would rather assert the need to exist than to demonstrate the efficacy of their techniques, and the list goes on of people who feel the need to be intentionally provocative.

A young advocate for social justice named Derecka Purnell once asked me, "How do you balance your research on Black male achievement with a possible decrease in urgency to help Black boys?" My response was, "Urgency based on hyperbole and conjecture *should* decrease. Urgency based on truth and compassion will endure."

REFERENCES

Beck, A. J. (2000). *Prison and jail inmates at midyear 1999* (NCJ Publication No. 181643). Washington, DC: U.S. Department of Justice.

Howerton, J. (2012). *Obama-Backer Charles Barkley talks guns with Bob Costas: 'I carry a gun' because 'I just feel safer with it.'* Retrieved from https://www.theblaze.com/stories/2012/12/05/charles-barkley-talks-guns-with-bob-costas-i-carry-a-gun-because-i-just-feel-safer-with-it

Justice Policy Institute. (2012). *Release: JPI stands by data in 2002 on education and incarceration* [Press release]. Retrieved from http://www.justicepolicy.org/news/4458

Kesssler, G. (2007). Young Black males headed for extinction? *Washington Post*. Retrieved from http://voices.washingtonpost.com/fact-checker/2007/10/young_black_males_headed_for_e_1.html

Knapp, L. G., Kelly-Reid, J. E., & Ginder, S. A. (2010). *Postsecondary institutions and price of attendance in the United States: Fall 2009 and degrees and other awards conferred: 2008–2009, and 12-month enrollment 2008–2009* (NCES 2011-250). Washington, DC: National Center for Education Statistics. Retrieved from http://nces.ed.gov/pubsearch

Ruggles, S., Sobek, M., Alexander, T., Fitch, C. A., Goeken, R., Hall, P. K., … Ronnander, C. (2009). *Integrated public use microdata series: Version 4.0* [Machine-readable database]. Minneapolis, MN: Minnesota Population Center.

Toldson, I. A. (2008). *Breaking barriers: Plotting the path to academic success for school-age African American males.* Washington, DC: Congressional Black Caucus Foundation.

U.S. Department of Education's National Center for Education Statistics. (2012). *The Integrated Postsecondary Education Data System (IPEDS)*. Retrieved from https://nces.ed.gov/ipeds/about-ipeds

West, H. C. (2010). *Prison inmates at midyear 2009–statistical tables*. Washington, DC: Bureau of Justice Statistics. Retrieved from http://www.bjs.gov/content/pub/pdf/pim09st.pdf

Ziedenberg, J., & Schiraldi, V. (2002). *Cellblocks or classrooms? The funding of higher education and corrections and its impact on African American men*. Retrieved from http://www.justicepolicy.org/research/2046Schoorman

BLACK STUDENTS DON'T READ

When standardized tests miss the mark.

***

In the U.S., Black and Hispanic students carry the burden of scoring lower on almost every known measure of achievement or aptitude than whites and Asians. These tests often serve as gatekeepers to specialized schools, gifted classes, and elite colleges – or, at the opposite end of the spectrum, as determinants of special education, grade repetition, and emotional-support classes.

Some parents, who may have a low-scoring son or daughter, often recoil from any attempts to challenge the merits of tests, and instead blame the schools for inadequately preparing their children. The schools respond by blaming the parents. When explaining the "achievement gap," test companies blame social inequities and cultural depravation (e.g., single-parent households and poverty) (Educational Testing Services, 2012). And the cyclical blame game continues, with solutions for Black students' progress an afterthought.

FAILING BLACK STUDENTS

When reporting on the achievement gap, the media have largely ignored the more complex issues regarding the merits of testing, such as bias and fairness, choosing instead to accept the tests at face value. To illustrate, let's examine how and why, over the last two years, many media outlets have been reporting that nearly 90 percent of Black children from elementary school through high school graduation, lack reading proficiency.

Late last year, researchers at Harvard released the report Globally Challenged: Are U.S. Students Ready to Compete? which highlighted gaps between races within the U.S. as well as between the U.S. and 65 countries that participated in the Program for International Student Assessment (Peterson, Woessmann, Hanushek, & Lastra-Anadon, 2011). For one section of the report, the team of four White research scholars removed all minority participants from their analysis because they found it "worth inquiring as to whether differences between the United States and other countries are attributable to the substantial minority population within the United States" (pp. 10–11).

The report inspired coverage from Black media outlets, including BET. com, which published an article with this telling headline: "Report: Only 13 Percent of 2011 Black Graduates Proficient in Reading" (Wright, 2011). The Harvard study found that less than half of White graduates were proficient in reading (40 percent), but this low percentage may matter little to those who consider White students to be the nation's benchmark.

Similarly, in 2010, the Council of the Great City Schools (CGCS) found that only 12 percent of Black fourth-grade boys were proficient in reading, compared with 38 percent of White boys (Lewis, Simon, Uzzell, Horwitz, & Casserly, 2010), as reported in the New York Times article, "Proficiency of Black students is found to be far lower than expected" (Gabriel, 2010). More disconcerting, however, is a tacit approval of measures concluding that almost 90 percent of Black people lack reading proficiency.

Who's asking questions like, "How are they measuring reading proficiency?" "Are the tests valid and culturally fair?" "How, and in what conditions, are they administering the tests?" and "How is it possible to have any Black publications if almost 90 percent of the Black population can't read?" Instead, these tests seem only to reinforce something we think we already know about Black people. We've all heard the adage, "If you ever want to keep anything away from a Black person, hide it in a book."

SEPARATING TESTS FROM TEST TAKERS

Imagine that your fourth-grade son is randomly selected to take a test of reading proficiency. He is given little information about the purpose of the assessment but can reasonably conclude that the test will not influence his grades or grade promotion at his current school. To test his level of reading comprehension, he is given a two-page passage about bees (National Center for Educational Statistics, 2009). Although he can read every word, the passage is extremely boring to him. Because the test is timed, he has to use a particular style of reading that feels contrived. At the end, he has to answer a series of questions, which have many plausible answers. In general, attributes like imagination and creativity work against him because the test requires him to be literal and deductive.

Such is the experience of children who take the National Assessment of Educational Progress (NAEP). Both the CGCS report and the Harvard study used NAEP assessment data to find that 88 percent of fourth-grade Black boys and 87 percent of all Black 12th-graders lack reading proficiency.

Hopefully, this background will lead you to be at least somewhat skeptical about reports that present highly inflated percentages of Black people who lack reading proficiency. We cannot deny the literacy problems in the Black community; however, I'm convinced that the problem lies less with children and more with the lack of understanding among adults of multiple literacies.

Confessions of a Bad Test Taker

Although I have never been formally diagnosed, I am certain that I met the diagnostic criteria for attention deficit hyperactivity disorder as a child and ADD as an adult. When I was in the fourth grade, my teacher assigned me to a "slow readers" group, based on tests and my teacher's subjective ratings. Today, I clearly remember the shame of being in a small group, with small, dumbed-down textbooks – a clear demarcation of the class based on ability.

Neither my mother nor I could make much sense of the deterioration of my academic progress and behavior at the time. I was making D's and F's on my report card and my teacher paddling me for reasons that I honestly can't fully remember. I do remember often being in my own mental space, making up stories in which I gave numbers a gender and personality during mathematics class, and making human figures and characters from basically any object (e.g., pencils and paper) I could manipulate.

I passed the fourth grade, but my spirit was broken. I had just left a teacher who clearly saw me as academically inept and started in a new class with a new teacher who seemed to feel the same way. It was a private school that my mother determined was not worth the cost.

I transferred to a public school, where I joined Ms. Law's fifth-grade class. Admittedly, my behavior became much more subdued at the public school. But early on, it became apparent that Ms. Law believed I was smart – genius smart, which perplexed my mother and me.

Notwithstanding Ms. Law's impression of my aptitude, I continued to have severe problems with boredom and drifting off when reading or paying attention in class. However, she certainly gave me the confidence to try my best. Throughout middle school and into high school, I used a combination of academic, social and survival skills to maintain grades that were usually slightly above the average of my peers.

My experiences are related to those of rising Louisiana fifth-grader Le'Brandole Green. His story is different because, unlike me, Le'Brandole

45

made nearly all A's in the fourth grade. However, when he sought admission to Faith Academy through a voucher program, the school administered a test that determined that Le'Brandole should repeat the fourth grade (McCormick, 2012). I've determined, through my analysis of the High School Longitudinal Study of 2009 (Ingels et al., 2011), that 18 percent of Black male students have had to repeat a grade by the time they reach ninth grade – apparently even those who make straight A's.

In Florida, Edlexander Rabassa, a sophomore at Colonial High School in Orlando, performed exceptionally in Advanced Placement classes and earned college credits before finishing high school. Yet, he failed the reading competency exam required to graduate. Apparently, Edlexander is in good company. Orange County School Board member Rick Roach has two master's degrees, yet he failed the state test for reading comprehension (Winerip, 2010).

LEARNING HOW TO READ

The Isis Papers, a collection of essays in which Frances Cress Welsing theorizes about a global system of White supremacy (Welsing, 1991), was the first book I read cover to cover. I was in the 11th grade and never thought I was the type of person who could read "big books." But it was a book of my own choosing, and I read it in a manner that felt natural to me. When reading, I often skipped ahead, then worked backward – making connections throughout the book with less rigid focus on the sequence of the pages.

This method of reading helped me process information but did little to help me perform better on tests. My ACT scores were so low that my scorecard stated that I had about a 15 percent probability of graduating from my eventual alma mater, Louisiana State University.

To make matters worse, because of my low performance on LSU's precollege assessment, I had to take a remedial reading course. I attended LSU through a minority Summer Bridge Program, with plans to transfer after the summer, because I believed what the experts said about my ACT scores.

Luckily, that summer I got a job preparing student records at the university's Junior Division, where I looked at hundreds of ACT scores paired with students' college transcripts. This exercise helped me conclude that my ACT scores did not have to mean what the experts said they meant.

In addition, I used the services of the school's Learning Assistance Center, which was an obscure and underused campus resource for students who were brave enough to admit they had learning challenges. The center taught me that I was forcing myself to read in a way that was unnatural to me. The methods that I used to read The Isis Papers were the methods I should have been using to read my biology textbooks. I also learned how to concept-map because I am more of a holistic thinker.

With that guidance, I elevated my performance in school so much that LSU waived a remedial reading requirement. I graduated in four years, completed a master's degree at Penn State University, received my Ph.D. from Temple University at the age of 28, and ultimately became editor-in-chief of The Journal of Negro Education.

MAKING A DIFFERENCE

I've shared some unflattering aspects of my past because I believe that the inferences that adults are making about tests are abating the intellectual and personal development of millions of children. If not for a few people who cared less about a statistic and more about "a person with a name," I would not have achieved any success in life.

The same is true for the children and emerging adults within our sphere of influence who are burdened with statistics that cheapen their existence. They need someone to tell them that they are good at something. They need schools like Loyola Academy in St. Louis, Mo., where Black male middle-school students can select some of the books they study from. Or schools like Urban Prep in Chicago, which has placed 100 percent of its Black male graduates in college since opening in 2006 (Ahmed-Ullah, 2012). However, Urban Prep's record does little to quiet test hawks who have minimized its success by citing low ACT scores (Klonsky, 2010).

According to my independent analysis of the High School Longitudinal Study of 2009 for the U.S. Department of Education Office of Special Education Programs, Black males are the most likely to take special education classes and the least likely to be in honors classes. Today, 9.1 percent of Black male high school students are in special education, compared with the national average of 6.5 percent; and 14.5 percent of Black males are in honors classes, compared with the national average of 25.6 percent (Ingels et al., 2011). Yes, there are more Black males in honors classes than in special education.

Nearly 1 in 10 Black boys have been diagnosed with ADHD, surpassed only by White boys at 13 percent. Among the 9.1 percent of Black boys who have been diagnosed with ADHD, 33 percent are in special education and 12 percent are in honors classes (Toldson, 2014). Yes, Black boys with disabilities could end up in honors classes.

What's the difference between a Black boy with ADHD who ends up in honors classes and those who end up in special education? It has less to do with the differences among the children and more to do with the difference makers they encounter – difference makers like Tim King at Urban Prep, H. Eric Clark at Loyola Academy and my fifth-grade teacher, Ms. Law.

Why Public Schools Are Confused – An Afterthought

The State: Why can't you be more like private schools?

Public school: What do you mean?

The State: I mean their students are learning, well behaved, and go on to do great things when they finish school. Your students don't seem to be learning anything.

Public school: OK, I'll see what I can do.

[After studying private schools]

Public school: I got it! We will extend the lunch period and enhance physical education. We believe that happy learners are the best learners. We will deemphasize learning drills and focus on activities that enrich our students' learning experience. We will have them maintain gardens, engage in creative writing and participate in exercises that spur critical thinking skills and instill a sense of agency.

Teachers will be encouraged to meet students where they are, but also set high expectations. Their priority will be to establish an atmosphere of care and respect. We will also locate EVERY alumnus who has done anything positive with their lives and have them speak to our students.

We are also going to stop teaching to the test. We will work with scholars in our network to develop our own diagnostics, but we will essentially ignore the results of any state assessment. And we will NEVER reveal ANY assessment scores to our students because that leaves them vulnerable to low self-esteem. We will use the scores for internal purposes only to enhance our curriculum – the scores of our tests that is, not the ones that you've developed. No offense.

I believe these modifications will make us a lot more like private schools.

The State: You're not in compliance. I'm shutting you down.

Public school: I'm confused.

The State: Yes, you are confused. That's why your students aren't learning anything. Why can't you be more like private schools?

REFERENCES

Ahmed-Ullah, N. S. (2012). Another perfect college acceptance year at urban prep. *Chicago Tribune*. Retrieved from http://articles.chicagotribune.com/2012-03-30/news/ct-met-urban-prep-20120330_1_students-graduate-graduation-rate-urban-prep-academy

Educational Testing Services. (2012). *Achievement gap research*. Retrieved from http://www.ets.org/s/achievement_gap/research/index.html

Gabriel, T. (2010). Proficiency of Black students is found to be far lower than expected. *The New York Times*. Retrieved from http://www.nytimes.com/2010/11/09/education/09gap.html?_r=0

Ingels, S. J., Pratt, D. J., Herget, D. R., Burns, L. J., Dever, J. A., Ottem, R., ... Leinwand, S. (2011). *High School Longitudinal Study of 2009 (HSLS:09). Base-year data file documentation (NCES 2011–328)*. Retrieved from http://nces.ed.gov/pubsearch

Klonsky, M. (2010). *Winners and losers in race to the top*. Retrieved from http://michaelklonsky.blogspot.com/2010/03/winners-losers-in-race-to-top.html

Lewis, S., Simon, C., Uzzell, R., Horwitz, A., & Casserly, M. (2010). *A call for change: The social and educational factors contributing to the outcomes of Black males in urban schools*. Retrieved from Washington, DC: The Council of the Great City Schools. Retrieved from http://www.edweek.org/media/black_male_study.pdf

McCormick, B. H. (2012). Mom questions ruling from voucher program. *The Baton Rouge Advocate*. Retrieved from http://theadvocate.com/news/3517739-123/transfer-and-repeat

National Center for Educational Statistics. (2009). *Reading sample questions: Grade 4*. Retrieved from http://nces.ed.gov/nationsreportcard/nies/nies_2009/sampquest_read.asp

Peterson, P. E., Woessmann, L., Hanushek, E. A., & Lastra-Anadon, C. X. (2011). *Globally challenged: Are U.S. students ready to compete?* Retrieved from http://www.hks.harvard.edu/pepg/PDF/Papers/PEPG11-03_GloballyChallenged.pdf

Toldson, I. A. (2014). *Decreasing dropout rates for African American male youth with disabilities*. Clemson, SC: National Dropout Prevention Center for Students with Disabilities. Retrieved from https://files.eric.ed.gov/fulltext/ED575729.pdf

Welsing, F. C. (1991). *The Isis papers: The keys to the colors*. Chicago, IL: Third World Press.

Winerip, M. (2010). Backtracking on Florida exams flunked by many, even an educator. *The New York Times*. Retrieved from http://www.nytimes.com/2012/06/11/education/florida-backtracks-on-standardized-state-tests.html?_r=3pagewanted=all&

Wright, D. (2011). *Report: Only 13 percent of 2011 Black graduates proficient in reading*. Retrieved from http://www.bet.com/news/national/2011/08/23/report-only-13-percent-of-2011-black-graduates-proficient-in-reading.html

BLACK STUDENTS ARE DROPPING OUT

You don't need to know the dropout rate to make a difference, but you should know it if you're going to make a statement.

***

On Bladensburg Road along the border of Prince Georges County, MD and Washington, DC, a billboard reads, "57% of District of Columbia students drop out." The billboard is large and imposing; with an orange backdrop and bold diagonal dashes on each side to mimic a road hazard sign. Many would find the content of the sign to be consistent with the frequently cited report, "The Urgency of Now" by the Schott Foundation, which states that Washington DC has a graduation rate of 38 percent for Black males (Schott Foundation for Public Education, 2012).

Figure 5.1. Picture of a billboard in Prince Georges County, MD

© KONINKLIJKE BRILL NV, LEIDEN, 2019 | DOI:10.1163/9789004397040_005

To be blunt, the message on the billboard is a lie, and technically, the percent of students that drop out has only a little to do with the percent that graduate. Yes, this is counterintuitive, but I will elaborate later. The high school dropout rate in DC is less than ten percent for all students and 14 percent for Black males (Toldson, 2014). The Schott Foundation's observation that the graduation rate for Black males is 38 percent is accurate. However, since most people do not know the difference between the graduation rate and dropout rate, the report is misrepresented far more than it is accurately presented. Anyone doing a pedestrian analysis of demographic trends in the DMV area understands that any measure of cohort graduation rates will be influenced by the outmigration of Black people from the city core.

Across the nation, most parents of school children are bombarded with dropout and graduation statistics that are very upsetting. The numbers as typically presented imply that either the public school system is woefully inadequate in meeting the educational needs of Black students, or Black students have incredible problems adjusting to a normal school environment. Many parents of students will respond to these numbers by removing their child from the school system, inadvertently making the numbers worse. When a child leaves a high school to attend a school in another district before they graduate, the graduation rate for the entire district goes down.

Civic leaders in Washington, DC should be concerned about the quality of education for all, the availability of affordable housing, and many other issues. However, civic leaders who believe that 62 percent of Black males, and 57 percent of all teenagers and young adults, are out of school and on the streets without a high school diploma will probably promote misguided practices, blaming, stigmatizing, and extreme agendas.

WHAT IS THE DIFFERENCE BETWEEN A GRADUATION RATE AND A DROPOUT RATE?

This is the boring technical stuff that is not fun to read, but essential to understand graduation rates and dropout rates. Independent analyses of graduation rates, such as The Schott 50 State Report on Public Education and Black Males, estimate graduation rates by dividing the number of students receiving diplomas by the number of students beginning high school four years earlier. This method yields a national graduation rate of 47 percent for Black males and 78 percent for White males (Schott Foundation for Public Education, 2012).

The National Center for Education Statistics (NCES) tracks dropout rates for the U.S. population using the Current Population Survey (CPS).

The "event dropout" rate refers to the percentage of 15 through 24-year-olds in the United States who withdrew from grades 10–12 within the last 12-month period. The NCES estimates the current event dropout rates for Black students to be 6.4 percent, compared to 2.3 for White students (U.S. Department of Education, 2018).

NCES uses the CPS to provide an estimate of the "status" dropout by surveying the proportion of the population that is between the ages of 16 and 24, not enrolled in school, and who have not earned a high school diploma or graduate equivalent. The current "status dropout" rate for Black males is 8.7 percent, compared to 5.4 percent for White males and 19.9 percent for Hispanic males (U.S. Department of Education, 2018).

IS THERE A DROPOUT CRISIS AMONG BLACK MALES?

In the context of education, most people who use the word "crisis" are either victims of propaganda or being intentionally hyperbolic to sell a point or an agenda. There are many educational issues that need to be resolved for the Black community, but there is an inherent danger in propagating a high school dropout crisis.

For instance, according to the Schott Foundation report only 28 percent of Black males graduate, which many interpret to imply that 72 percent of Black males are dropping out of New York City schools. This would indeed be a crisis. Imagine 72 percent of the city's young Black males being out of school and on the streets. In raw numbers, this would mean that about 155,000 Black males in New York City between the ages of 16 and 24 are high school dropouts, with the remaining less than 61,000 in high school or college or finishing any type of diploma or degree program. How scary does this sound? This is scary enough for someone to support any extreme agenda, from the complete privatization of public schools to "stop-and-frisk."

When we use the Current Population Survey to estimate the number of Black males in the New York City metro area between the ages of 16 and 24 who are not in school and have not completed high school, the percentage of the total population of Black males in that age range is around 15 percent.

Meanwhile, insidious practices in New York City are creating a racial caste system in education. While Black people are supporting inept dropout prevention programs, the school system is keeping Black students from specialized high schools, like Bronx High School of Science and Brooklyn

Tech by creating an arcane testing criterion. They are also eliminating advanced mathematics and science classes from schools with the largest percentage of Black students. The school system eliminates the possibility that many Black students can earn a Regents diploma, because of the curriculum they offer.

In fact, the primary reason that the Schott Foundation's number for New York is so absurdly low is not because Black males are dropping out. It is because they are not earning Regents diplomas (Fertig, 2010). This should change just about everything about how we are currently addressing the 72 percent of Black males who did not make the Schott Foundation's cut in New York City.

What Are We Doing to Make Sure Black Children Know the Truth about Themselves?

I was honored to receive an invitation from Reverend Al Sharpton to serve on a panel for the National Action Network. On the panel, Steve Perry admonished the public school system by saying that 50% of Black males do not graduate. Later the Rev. Al Sharpton said on MSNBC that only 52% of Black males graduate on time.

The often-stated notion that more than half of Black males drop out, or do not graduate, is not true. Cohort graduation rate calculations miss students who graduate late, graduate early, obtain a GED, or transfer to schools outside of their district. None of this information should be construed to minimize the importance of collective action to promote Black male achievement. Putting this information in perspective, we should acknowledge that completion rates for Black males continue to lag behind White males.

This chapter describes how widespread recitals and simplistic representations of very complex calculations of the dropout rate and graduation rate are creating more problems than solutions for Black males. People simply should not use the statistic if they do not understand how any given statistic is derived. And people who know the truth but continue to distort and sensationalize the problem through statistics because they want people to pay attention to them, are a part of the problem.

Earlier this year, Adam Eugene, a sophomore at Destrahen High School in New Orleans told me, "Dr. Toldson, we have been hearing negative things about ourselves all of our lives. This is the first time that we are hearing that the news about us isn't all bad. A lot of times, when children hear negative things, they start to believe they can't learn and give up. So, my question is:

54

What are you doing to make sure children much younger than us hear the truth about themselves?"

What are we doing?

RELATED ISSUES

Dropout vs. Putout

I just got access to the raw data for the first follow up of the High School Longitudinal Survey, and I'm starting to analyze the data (N = 23,415).

Alarming finding: Among students who dropped out of high school, 33% of Black students left because they were suspended or expelled, compared to 19% for White students and 13% for Hispanic students.

Most of the times, when we attempt to address the so-called "dropout crisis" we focus on Black students' motivation for dropping out. Maybe we need to start focusing on schools' intentions for putting them out. (Toldson, 2013)

A First Look at Black Fall 2009 Ninth-Graders in 2012

In a national survey conducted by the U.S. Department of Education, National Center for Education Statistics, 87 percent of Black students who were in the 9th grade in 2009 were in the 11th grade by 2012. The percent that fell behind but remained in school was 1.5 and 4.3 percent dropped out of school. The percent that was skipped ahead or graduated early was 7.4 percent. Therefore, Black students were more likely to advance than fall behind or drop out.

About 60 percent of Black high school students expect to eventually graduate from college, which is comparable to students in other racial groups. However, Black students are behind their peers in the percent who are taking college preparatory classes. Fifty-three percent of Asian students, 24 percent of White students, 16 percent of Hispanic students, and 12 percent of Black students are taking precalculus or calculus by the 11th grade.

Therefore we need less dropout prevention programs and more Public reciprocity in educating for postsecondary success (PREPS) (Toldson, 2013; Toldson & Lewis, 2012).

REFERENCES

Fertig, B. (2010). Study finds New York has lowest grad rate for Black males. *WNYC*. Retrieved from https://www.wnyc.org/story/91282-study-finds-new-york-has-lowest-grad-rate-black-males/

Schott Foundation for Public Education. (2012). *Black lives matter: Schott 50 state report on public education and Black males*. Retrieved from http://blackboysreport.org/

Toldson, I. A. (2013). *In Facebook*. Retrieved December 12, 2018, from https://www.facebook.com/ivory.toldson/posts/10100385345172070

Toldson, I. A. (2014). *Building bridges: Connecting out-of-school time to classroom success among school-age Black males in the District of Columbia*. Washington, DC: The DC Children and Youth Investment Trust Corporation.

Toldson, I., A., & Lewis, C. W. (2012). Public Reciprocity in Education for Postsecondary Success (PREPS) for students of color: The legal justification and a call for action (Editor's Commentary). *The Journal of Negro Education, 81*(1), 1–9. doi:10.7709/jnegroeducation.81.1.0001

U.S. Department of Education. (2018). *The condition of education 2018* (NCES 2018-144). Washington, DC: National Center for Education Statistics. Retrieved from https://nces.ed.gov/pubsearch/pubsinfo.asp?pubid=2018144

SINGLE PARENTS CAN'T RAISE BLACK CHILDREN

What if the single parent was White?

***

Do Black children have natural disadvantages in school because most are from single-parent homes? Several years ago, before his conviction for sexual assault, comedian and actor, Bill Cosby, chided the "apathy" he observed among Black parents (Roberts, 2007). He, like many others, believes that the fading presence of the Black nuclear family places Black children at a social disadvantage, and creates a burden on society.

The link between father absence and community dissonance among Black people was postulated almost 50 years ago in the U.S. Department of Labor's Moynihan report (Ziegler, 1995). Since then, the percent of Black children being raised in single-parent homes has grown from 20 percent to 70 percent. In the United States, 31 percent of Black children have both a mother and a father in the home; 53 percent have only a mother present; 7 percent have only a father present; and 9 percent have neither parent present.[1] These figures have been represented in various ways in the media to portray a single-parent crisis in the Black community.

At 28 percent, the percent of White children in single-parent homes has grown to exceed the figure that initially caused Senator Moynihan's consternation for Black families in 1965. In fact, The United States has nearly 4 million more White children in single-parent households than Black children. If White families did not have children out of wedlock, divorce, or abandon their children, the total population of children in single-parent, and no-parent, homes would reduce by nearly 40 percent.

By comparison, Black people account for 25 percent of the total population of children in single-parent homes. The percentage of Black children in single-parent homes is more than three times higher than the percentage of Whites. However, in the context of social impact, total incidents are unequivocally more important than within group percentages.

I make these observations not to deflect responsibility or to be contentious, but to: First, challenge the narrative that single-parent households among Black people are the most common in society; and second, question the audacity of people from outside of the Black community to criticize Black families, while ignoring their own race's contributions to their perceived social ills. No White person has the standing, or moral authority, to question the household composition of Black households. If single-parent homes are a burden to the United States, White families account for the heaviest drag of all races.

However, I did not write this chapter to advocate for sharing the burden of single-parent homes. Rather, the purpose of this chapter is to assess the premise that single-parent homes are a burden. Across all races, the United States has more than 27.7 million children who currently reside in single-parent, or no-parent (children in state custody, and those being raised by nonparent guardians) homes. For this chapter, I examine the educational prospects of children being raised in nontraditional family units. In the second part of this book, I review what schools and communities can do to support Black parents in general.

DO BLACK CHILDREN FROM TWO-PARENT HOMES PERFORM BETTER IN SCHOOL?

In a superficial view of the numbers, Black children from two-parent households have academic advantages over Black children from single-parent homes. For example, the National Household Education Surveys (NHES)-Parent and Family Involvement Survey found that Black students from two-parent homes reported an average GPA of 3.1, those from mother-only homes reported a 3.0, father-only homes reported a 2.9, and no-parent homes reported a 2.7 (Toldson, 2008).

I also used Health Behaviors in School-age Children (HBSC) to determine the impact of fathers on the academic success of young Black males. Among Black male middle and high school students who had a father present, 62 percent reported good or very good grades, compared to 55 percent for students with no father present. Among the students who reported not having their mother or father in the home, fewer than half reported making good or very good grades in school (Toldson, 2008).

Finally, I used the American Community Survey to determine whether household composition had an impact on Black males' persistence through grade school. About 7.7 percent of Black males from two-parent homes were severely off-track (more than two grade levels behind) by the time they reached the 9th grade, compared with 10.6 percent among those from mother-headed households (Ruggles et al., 2009).

Interestingly, Black males in households with only a mother were significantly more likely to be on-track academically than Black males in households with a father only. Contrarily, Black females in households with a father only were more likely to be academically on track than those in households with a mother only. Black children from households with neither a mother nor a father were twice as likely to be severely off-track when compared with Black children from two- and one-parent households.

As a single variable, household composition carries little weight and appears to serve as a proxy for more serious issues, such as teenage pregnancy and incarcerated parents. In analyses, a myriad of co-variants (e.g., parents' education and parent practices) nullify the effects of household composition on academic progress cited in the previous section. For example, in my analysis of the *High School Longitudinal Survey*, a Black student from a two-parent household with just one parent who dropped out of high school was three times more likely to repeat a grade in school than a student from a single-parent household where the primary caregiver had an associate's degree or higher (Toldson, 2008).

Moving Forward

In many ways, the focus on single-parent households has distracted us from more legitimate indicators of risk and have created disobliging attitudes toward Black parents and students. Although a larger number of White children from single-parent homes exist, many argue that the impact is not as severe because single White mothers typically receive more child support and alimony than single Black mothers.

While this is a fair assessment, it is important not to confuse affluence with responsibility. Paying a part-time nanny to pick up your child from school so you can work late, hiring a tutor when your child makes a C in mathematics, and paying for test prep classes does not make a parent more responsible – it makes them more financially capable. By contrast, I admire and empathize with the single parents who spend hours and days fighting schools who try to suspend their child under misguided zero-tolerance policies; teachers who give unsolicited and unqualified mental health diagnoses; and administrators who try to track their children into special education classes.

We often overstate and exaggerate the drawbacks of being raised by a single parent. At the same time, we ignore the real and persistent disadvantages of the nearly one million Black children being raised by noncustodial parents. In addition, without much evidence, context, or specificity, we make sweeping assumptions about why Black boys need a father in the home. At the same time, we ignore the vital role that Black fathers play in the lives of daughters and that Black mothers play in the lives of sons.

We will never fully understand the contributions of Black parents through pedestrian analyses, stereotypes, arrogance, and condescension. Frequent communication with parents helps us to support a variety of people who want more for their children than they ever had, even if they don't fully understand what that means or how to get there.

Single Parents and Incarceration – Response to a Message

Hello Dr. Toldson, I just read a 2013 article you wrote for the Root – Single Parents Aren't the Problem. I was wondering if you knew what the percentage of incarcerated African Americans raised in single-parent homes is? I'm having a debate with a colleague. Can you help me out? – Derek

Hi Derek: You're not going to find a clean stat for that question. The incarcerated population includes an annual headcount of people in state and federal prisons and local jails. At any given count, you have people in jail for hopping the turnstile at a subway, to serial killers. Also, the incarcerated population includes a wide variation of ages. Generally, older people in the U.S. are more likely to have grown up in 2-parent homes, irrespective of criminal disposition.

The Black juvenile arrests rate and the percent of Black children being raised in single-parent homes both began to rise in the 1980s. However, while juvenile arrests plummeted in the mid-90s and have trended downward ever since, the percent of children being raised in single-parent homes continued to increase. The number of Black juvenile arrests and single-parent homes has been trending in opposite directions for nearly 30 years.

I would suspect that the percent of all incarcerated adults who were raised in single-parent homes is high. But it's not a cause and effect relationship. I was raised in a single-parent home, but nothing about the singleness of my mother left me vulnerable to incarceration. Her in-home parenting, and my nonresident father, easily pointed me to college.

Marriage rates are lower among lesser educated and lower income populations. Nothing suggests that lack of marriage leads to less education and lower income. In fact, the opposite is true. People who are poor have more difficulties managing a variety of social conventions, including getting and staying married. All of us who are married can agree that healthy finances make marriage less stressful.

There are a variety of childhood circumstances that independently predict adult criminal behavior, including abuse, neglect, mental illness, cognitive dysfunction, rejection from peers, and early criminal exposure. Single parents with even modest incomes and levels of education, or who have adequate support systems, have no trouble raising children who do not commit crime.

Bottom line, household composition does not independently predict criminal behavior and has no impact when controlling the factors that really matter. – Ivory

NOTE

[1] For all statistical analyses, unless otherwise noted, I used the Integrated Public Use Microdata Series (IPUMS), which consists of 66 high-precision samples of the U.S. population drawn from 16 federal censuses, and the American Community Surveys (ACS) of 2000–2011. The data come from Ruggles S., Alexander J.T., Genadek K., Goeken R., Schroeder M.B., Sobek M. (2011). Integrated Public Use Microdata Series: Version 5.0 (machine-readable database), Minneapolis: University of Minnesota.

REFERENCES

Roberts, R. (2007). Bill Cosby's mission. *Good Morning America (ABC)*, 1.

Ruggles, S., Sobek, M., Alexander, T., Fitch, C. A., Goeken, R., Hall, P. K., … Ronnander, C. (2009). *Integrated public use microdata series: Version 4.0* [Machine-readable database]. Minneapolis, MN: Minnesota Population Center.

Toldson, I. A. (2008). *Breaking barriers: Plotting the path to academic success for school-age African American males*. Washington, DC: Congressional Black Caucus Foundation.

Ziegler, D. (1995). Single parenting: A visual analysis. In B. J. Dickerson (Ed.), *African American single mothers: Understanding their lives and families* (pp. 80–93). Thousand Oaks, CA: Sage Publications.

SMART BLACK STUDENTS ARE ACTING WHITE

Black children don't need to redefine "acting White," they need us to redefine "acting Black."

***

Do Black students purposefully underachieve because they attribute being smart to 'acting White?' For more than a decade, academics, policymakers, and cultural critics have publicly chided Black children for having an anti-intellectual attitude, based on the "Acting White Theory."

The Acting White Theory originated in the 1980s with Dr. John Ogbu's ethnographic research and is commonly used to explain present day 'achievement gaps' between Black and White students (Ogbu, 2004). Today, the Acting White Theory has its own Wikipedia entry, and was mentioned by then-Senator Barack Obama in 2004, when he said, "Children can't achieve unless we raise their expectations and turn off the television sets and eradicate the slander that says a Black youth with a book is acting White."

The Acting White Theory seems to have particular cachet among Black people who feel a certain disdain toward the less refined (pejoratively "ghetto") aspects of the Black community. Many of them have been called "sellouts," which reinforces a key tenant of the Acting White Theory. Other scholars, such as Dr. Edward Rhymes and Dr. Michael Eric Dyson push back against the theory. Dr. Rhymes stated in his blog, "Somehow many African Americans (usually the affluent, disconnected ones) have swallowed this misconception about African-American youth being anti-intellectual and anti-education. This ideology concerning nerds and geeks did not originate in the African-American community, but in predominantly White, middle-class, suburban communities" (Rhymes, 2002).

The Acting White Theory is difficult to assess through research. Many scholars who claim to find evidence of this theory loosely interpret their data and exploit the 'expert gap' to sell their findings. One of the best examples of this is Dr. Roland G. Fryer's research paper, "Acting White: The Social Price Paid by the Best and Brightest Minority Students" (Fryer, 2006).

© KONINKLIJKE BRILL NV, LEIDEN, 2019 | DOI:10.1163/9789004397040_007

Here Dr. Fryer uses the Add Health data[1] to demonstrate, in a nutshell, that the highest achieving Black students had fewer friends than high achieving Black students. In his study, Black students with a 3.5 GPA had the most friends of all academic levels, those with a 4.0 had about as many friends as those with about a 3.0, and those with less than a 2.5 had the fewest friends of all.

Overall, contrary to the study title, Dr. Fryer's research clearly demonstrated that the "social price" paid by the lowest achieving Black students is far greater than the so-called price paid by the highest achieving Black students. Moreover, methodologically the study must make the ostensible leap that the number of friends a Black student has is a direct measure a consequence of acting White. Interestingly, Dr. Fryer used the same mammoth dataset that Dr. Satoshi Kanazawa used to pseudo-scientifically "prove" that Black women (actually teenage girls) are less attractive (actually rated less attractive by adult raters of an unknown racial background) – but I digress (Britton, 2011).

Beyond the confirmation bias and social anecdotes, many studies, including a recent study by Dr. Tina Wildhagen in The Journal of Negro Education, disprove the Acting White Theory (Wildhagen, 2011). In my research, I have noticed a "nerd bend" among all races, whereby high, but not the highest, achievers receive the most social rewards (Toldson, 2011). For instance, the lowest achievers get bullied the most and bullying continues to decrease as grades increase, however when grades go from good to great, bullying starts to increase again slightly. Thus, the highest achievers get bullied more than high achievers, but significantly less than lowest achievers.

Another concept that is firmly established in educational research literature is the "attitude-achievement paradox" (Mickelson, 1990). For more than three decades, researchers have found that Black students consistently exhibit more positive attitudes about education than White students, contrary to their lower levels of academic achievement.

WHAT BLACK STUDENTS THINK ABOUT BEING SMART

To further examine evidence for the Acting White Theory, I analyzed raw data from a CBS News Monthly Poll (Toldson & Owens, 2010). This special topic poll surveyed more than 1,000 high school students nationwide on their perception of being smart and their opinions about smart students (i.e., students who study hard and receive good grades).

In the most pointed question, students were asked, "Thinking about the kids who get good grades in your school, which ONE best describes how you see them: (1) cool, (2) normal, (3) weird, (4) boring, or (5) admired?" Response differences between Black males, Black females, White males, and White females were not statistically different, however, at 17%, Black males were the most likely to consider such students as "cool." Among the other students, there were 11% to 12% who considered students who make good grades as "cool." The vast majority (about 60%) of all students, regardless of race or gender considered students who make good grades as "normal," and rarely considered them to be "weird" or "boring."

Another question asked, "In general, if you really did well in school, is that something you would be proud of and tell all your friends about or something you would be embarrassed about and keep to yourself?" Eighty-nine percent of all students said they would be "proud and tell all." At 95%, Black females were the most likely to be proud of doing well in school. At 17%, White males were the most likely to be "embarrassed or keep to self" or report that they "did not know." Corresponding feelings of embarrassment or dissonance for Black males was 10% and for 4% Black females.

The final question that related to feelings about being smart was, "In general, how would your friends react if you couldn't hang out because you were doing homework or studying for school? Would they (1) be supportive of you, (2) make fun of you or try to disrupt you, or (3) they wouldn't care one way or the other? At 45%, Black females were the most likely to say their friends would be supportive, with Black males and White females tied at 40%. White males were significantly lower. Only 24% of White males reported that their friends would be supportive.

WHAT BLACK STUDENTS THINK ABOUT COLLEGE

Consistent with other national surveys, the CBS Poll found that most Black students want to go the college. Across races, about 65% of males and 75% of females planned to go to a four-year college after graduating from high school. More Black student, regardless of gender, planned to go to vocational or technical school, and more male students, regardless of race, planned to go to the armed forces.

When responding to the question, "Would you say most of your friends probably will or probably will not go to college?" Black male and female students were significantly more likely to respond, "Will not." Forty percent of Black males and 31% of Black females stated that their friends probably would not go to college, compared to 23% of White males and females.

When asked the question, "What do you think your friends would like more: if you go to college, OR if you don't go to college, OR your friends would not care either way?" Black students were more likely to report that their friends wanted them to go to college. White students were more likely to state that their friends would not care either way.

Several factors were revealed that discouraged Black students from pursuing college. More than one-third of all Black students who decided not to attend college stated that they could not afford it. Ten percent of Black males stated that they did not have enough information about college. Fifteen percent of Black females elected not to go to college for "family reasons," compared to zero percent of Black males. Black females were the most likely to report being stressed about college when compared to other race groups.

WHAT BLACK STUDENTS NEED TO BE SUCCESSFUL IN SCHOOL

Schools

The CBS News Poll asked students, "In your school, which ONE of the following would do the most to help make your education better: (1) Smaller classes, (2) a safer school, (3) more individual attention from teachers, (4) courses that prepare you for the real world, (5) More help getting into college?" For Black students, the top choice was "courses that prepare you for the real world" and second was "more individual attention from teachers."

Teachers

The CBS News Poll asked students, "Overall, how would you rate the quality of your school's teachers? Would you say they are excellent, good, fair, or poor teachers?" Not surprising, our analysis found that Black students who rated their teachers as "excellent,' were also more likely to report good grades in school. This finding corresponds with results in Breaking Barriers, whereby high-achieving Black students reported that their teachers were interested in them "as a person," treated them fairly, encouraged them to express their views, and gave extra help when needed. Teachers who were effective also routinely let their students know when they did a good job (Toldson, 2008).

Safety

The CBS News Poll found equally low ratings of "a safer school" for Black and White students. However, analysis of the Breaking Barriers reports found that Black students were significantly less prone to feel safe at school when compared to White students. An analysis found a relationship between feeling safe at school and academic achievement for all students regardless of race. Neighborhood safety also significantly influenced academic success. When responding to the question, "Generally speaking, I feel safe in the area where I live," Black students who were reported high achievers were more likely to respond, "Always." However, Black students across levels of academic achievement felt less safe than White students.

Parents

In the CBS News Poll, Black and White students were similar in their ratings of receiving pressure from parents to study. However, Black students were less likely than White students to state that their parents place pressure on them to go to college. In Breaking Barriers, findings produced compelling evidence that modeling is an important component of academic development among Black males and females. Father's education, but not mother's education, had a significant impact on the academic achievement of Black males but not as much for Black females. The contrary was true for Black females, who demonstrated stronger academic achievement when their mothers had a college degree. Understanding these findings within the context of other ethnic groups provides further insights into possible reasons Black males are underperforming in schools. African American males were almost twice as likely to have a father who did not complete college as Asian Americans or European Americans.

Another aspect of parenting that had a significant impact on Black students' academic progress was a parent's involvement with school. When analyzing similar parenting practices with a separate dataset, the strongest parenting indicators of academic success were two holistic factors: (a) Parents who often told children they were proud of them; and (b) Parents who let students know when they did a good job. Interestingly, although probably important for other aspects of development, restricting children's behavior, such as time spent with friends or watching TV, did not produce significant effects on grades.

Conclusion

From these analyses of relevant research and large national datasets, we can conclude that the Acting White Theory for Black education is more fodder for cultural critics than a construct that will advance any meaningful solutions for academic achievement gaps. In many ways, White males are the most forthright about being apathetic toward educational values, which is likely attributed to having less of a need for impression management due to having no stereotype threat. For Black people, the context of "acting White" could be primarily a function of satire and sarcasm, and have more to do with styles of dress, communication nuances, music preferences, and a swagger that is independent of intellectual aptitude. The problem with the Acting White Theory is that it promotes the misconception that Black students underachieve because of their corrupted attitudes. Meanwhile, many Black students are relegated to under-resourced schools and lack motivation because of low expectations from teachers and school leaders, unfair discipline, and fewer opportunities for academic enrichment.

Overall, education is most effective when it promotes positive school-related growth experiences with emphasis on teacher–student relationships, didactic learning, and emotional support. Positive parent–child communication, including parents expressing praise, helping with homework, and cooperative parenting arrangements, also promotes academic success among Black students. It is critical that academic support and resources are provided to all students, particularly those from low-income areas. In addition, academic functioning and peer relations could improve through civic engagement, volunteerism, and sports. Most importantly, educators must advocate for policies that reduce racial disparities in income and increase equity and inclusion in education.

NOTE

[1] "Initiated in 1994 and supported by three program project grants from the Eunice Kennedy Shriver National Institute of Child Health and Human Development (NICHD) with co-funding from 23 other federal agencies and foundations, Add Health is the largest, most comprehensive longitudinal survey of adolescents ever undertaken. Beginning with an in-school questionnaire administered to a nationally representative sample of students in grades 7–12, the study followed up with a series of in-home interviews conducted in 1995, 1996, 2001–2002, and 2008. Other sources of data include questionnaires for parents, siblings, fellow students, and school administrators and interviews with romantic partners. Preexisting databases provide information about neighborhoods and communities" (https://www.cpc.unc.edu/projects/addhealth/about).

REFERENCES

Britton, K. (2011). The data are in regarding Satoshi Kanazawa. *Scientific American.* Retrieved from https://blogs.scientificamerican.com/guest-blog/the-data-are-in-regarding-satoshi-kanazawa/

Fryer, R. G. (2006). "Acting White": The social price paid by the best and brightest minority students. *Education Next, 6*(1), 52–59.

Mickelson, R. A. (1990). The attitude-achievement paradox among Black adolescents. *Sociology of Education, 63*(1), 44–61. doi:10.2307/2112896

Ogbu, J. U. (2004). Collective identity and the burden of "acting White" in Black history, community, and education. *Urban Review, 36*(1), 1–35.

Rhymes, E. (2002). *Acting White: African American students and education.* Retrieved from http://www.Blackcommentator.com/100/100_cover_acting_White.html

Toldson, I. A. (2008). *Breaking barriers: Plotting the path to academic success for school-age African American males.* Washington, DC: Congressional Black Caucus Foundation.

Toldson, I. A. (2011). *Breaking barriers 2: Plotting the path away from juvenile detention and toward academic success for school-age African American males.* Washington, DC: Congressional Black Caucus Foundation.

Toldson, I. A., & Owens, D. (2010). Editor's comment: 'Acting Black': What Black kids think about being smart and other school-related experiences. *Journal of Negro Education, 79*(2), 91–96.

Wildhagen, T. (2011). Testing the "acting White" hypothesis: A popular explanation runs out of empirical steam. *Journal of Negro Education, 80*(4), 445–463.

BLACK MALE TEACHERS ARE MISSING

Black male teachers don't need to help Black boys; they need to help White teachers help Black boys.

***

Many media sources have propagated the view that "Black male teachers are becoming extinct" (Huntspon & Howell, 2012). Currently, Black males represent less than 2 percent of the nation's teacher workforce. A recent article suggests that Black males are underrepresented in the teaching profession because they prefer to pursue more lucrative careers (Hare, 2013). Many also postulate that because Black males have had negative educational experiences, they are less likely to choose a career in education.

What are the consequences of Black males eluding a tacit moral obligation to teach? Several years back, CNN suggested that placing Black men in the classroom could be the answer to solving problems in the Black community such as gang violence, high school dropout rates, and fatherless homes (Harris, 2010). According to most reports, the lack of Black male teachers directly or indirectly results in abysmal deficiencies in the educational progress of Black males. It seems no coincidence that Black males are the least likely to be teachers as adults, but the most likely to drop out of school, get suspended, or perform poorly on standardized tests as students.

Unfortunately, this narrative on Black male teachers is based on supposition and stereotyping, not a careful analysis of the data. Males of all races are underrepresented in the U.S. teaching force. The percentage of White male P-12 students is twice the percent of White male teachers; the percentage of Black male students is more than three times the percent of Black male teachers; and the percentage of Hispanic male students is almost seven times the percentage of Hispanic male teachers. Asian males represent less than .5 percent of the teaching force.

© KONINKLIJKE BRILL NV, LEIDEN, 2019 | DOI:10.1163/9789004397040_008

BLACK MALE TEACHERS – SEPARATING FACTS FROM MYTHS

In 2013, Dr. Chance Lewis and I released an edited book entitled "Black Male Teachers: Diversifying the United States' Teacher Workforce" (Lewis & Toldson, 2013). In the book we suggest responsible methods for increasing the number and capacity of Black male teachers, without subjecting them to differential standards of success. In this chapter, I examine the myths used to explain the shortage of Black male teachers and why the purpose of diversifying the nation's teacher workforce should be to benefit the teaching profession, not individual students.

To begin, I offer a preliminary analysis to examine diversity within the teaching force, and among preschool through 12th grade (P-12) students, in the United States using the American Community Survey (ACS). The ACS is a nationwide survey designed to provide demographic, social, economic, and housing data for the nation, states, congressional districts, counties, places, and other localities every year (for information on the ACS visit www.census.gov/acs/www).

Today, of the more than 6 million teachers in the United States, nearly 80 percent are White, 9.6 percent are Black, 7.4 percent are Hispanic, 2.3 percent are Asian, and 1.2 percent is another race. Eighty percent of all teachers are female. Relative to the composition of P-12 students in the United States, the current teaching force lacks racial and gender diversity. This report provides commentary on the causes and consequences of having a majority White and female teaching force in a diverse school system, as well as strategies to improve diversity, equity, and inclusion among P-12 teachers and students.

Teachers comprise the largest professional occupation in the United States; accounting for the most professional employees among college-educated White women, Black women, and Black men. Despite the considerable number of teachers relative to other professions held by college educated Black men, they represent less than 2 percent of the teaching force, of a student body that is 7 percent Black male. By comparison, White female teachers comprise 63 percent of the teaching force, of a student body that is 27 percent White female. Considering the entire student body, the United States has one White female teacher for every 15 students and one Black male teacher for every 534 students. See Table 8.1 for a complete picture of the racial and gender diversity in the U.S. teaching force.

Males of all races are underrepresented in the U.S. teaching force. The percent of White male P-12 students is twice the percent of White male

Table 8.1. Preschool through 12th grade students in the United States by race and gender

	Preschool and Kindergarten	Elementary and middle	Secondary	Total	Percent
White male	2,683,523	9,341,655	5,019,202	17,044,380	29.15%
White female	2,490,077	8,795,371	4,724,365	16,009,813	27.38%
Hispanic male	1,004,956	3,655,710	1,705,159	6,365,825	10.89%
Hispanic female	961,659	3,449,045	1,620,313	6,031,017	10.32%
Black male	641,253	2,318,737	1,359,292	4,319,282	7.39%
Black female	602,753	2,208,981	1,302,542	4,114,276	7.04%
Asian male	220,511	696,654	353,993	1,271,158	2.17%
Asian female	213,176	679,030	327,046	1,219,252	2.09%
Other male	206,907	605,737	255,785	1,068,429	1.83%
Other female	203,517	567,032	254,257	1,024,806	1.75%
Total	**9,228,332**	**32,317,952**	**16,921,954**	**58,468,238**	**100%**

teachers; the percent of Black male students is more than three times the percent of Black male teachers; and the percent of Hispanic male students is almost seven times the percent of Hispanic male teachers. The overrepresentation of White female teachers may mitigate some issues associated with the lower number of White male teachers because they have cultural alignment with White males. However, irrespective of gender, Black and Hispanic teachers are underrepresented in the U.S. teaching force. Nationally, Black and Hispanic boys spend most of their school experiences under cross-gender and cross-cultural supervision. See Table 8.2 for a complete picture of the racial and gender diversity in the U.S school system.

Black Males Are NOT Avoiding the Teaching Profession Because They Are Less Altruistic and More Interested in Lucrative Careers

I conducted an analysis of the top 10 occupations among Black and White males who have at least a bachelor's degree. Primary school teacher was the number one profession of college educated Black men and number three for White men. Secondary school teacher was number five for Black men and number 14 for White men. Educational administrator was number six for Black men and number 20 for White men, and counselor was number seven for Black men and number 40 for White men.

The occupations that were in the top 10 for college educated White men, but not in the top ten for college educated Black men were lawyers, chief executives, sales representatives, and physicians and surgeons. Overall, higher paying occupations are more commonly held among White men, even when controlling for education. Black men who are college educated are far more likely to be a teacher or a range of other "helping professions."

Reasons for the Shortage of Black Male Teachers Are Diverse and Nuanced

Several reasons account for the dearth of Black male teachers. First, Black males are less likely to graduate from college. In the U.S. population, 16 percent of Black males and 19 percent of Black females have completed college. Second, Black males are less likely to major in education. In 2009, 7,603 Black males and 25,725 Black females graduated from college with a degree in education. Third, Black males who graduate with a degree in education are less likely to become a teacher. Only 23 percent of Black men with a degree in education become a P-12 teacher, compared to 27 percent for White men, 41 percent for Black women, and 42 percent for White women.

Interestingly, an upward mobility advantage within the field of education also appears to reduce the number of Black men in the classroom. Almost 7 percent of Black males with a degree in education become educational administrators, compared with 5 percent for Black females and White males, and only 2.8 percent for White females. If current trends in occupational choice stay the same, more Black men enrolling and graduating from college will naturally increase the number and percentage of Black male teachers, with complementary increases in Black male physicians, lawyers, engineers, nurses, bankers, brokers, and other professions.

No Evidence Suggests That Increasing the Number of Black Male Teachers Will Eliminate the Achievement Gap

Black male teachers are well represented in Memphis, where they represent 6.5 percent of the teaching force; more than three times the national average of 1.8 percent. They are scarce in Tallahassee, FL, where they represent less than one percent of the teaching force. Montgomery, AL has the highest percentage of Black male teachers. In this city with a population of 206,297 (71 percent Black), more than one in four (26 percent) of the teachers are Black males. However, most southern cities are more like Baton Rouge,

LA, which has a population of 439,013 (52 percent Black), and less than 1 percent of the teachers are Black males.

According to *The Schott Foundation for Public Education's 50 State Report on Public Education and Black Males* (Schott Foundation for Public Education, 2012), the graduation rate for Black males in Baton Rouge is 42 percent and the graduation rate for Black males in Montgomery is 33 percent. Notably, graduation rates for White males in both cities are less than the national average for Black males.

In the 10 metro areas with the largest number of Black people, New York, Chicago, Atlanta, Washington, Philadelphia, Detroit, Houston, Los Angeles-Long Beach, Dallas-Fort Worth, and Baltimore, Baltimore has the highest percentage of Black male teachers with 5.4 percent. Los Angeles and Detroit have the lowest with 2.3 percent. Notably, all of the large metro areas with a large Black population had a percentage of Black male teachers that was higher than the national average.

When connecting the cities to corresponding graduation rates as presented in *The Schott Foundation Report,* there is no compelling evidence that the presence of Black male teachers alone will improve graduation rates for Black males. However, let's keep this information within its proper perspective. Even in a district with a population consistent representation of Black male teachers, Black male students would have little interaction with Black male teachers. A Black male student, who has had about 55 teachers from K to 12th grade across all subjects, could expect to have had one Black male teacher in Detroit or three Black male teachers in Memphis – this isn't a system changing difference.

The Benefits of Black Male Teachers Can Only Be Realized through Their Relationship to the Teaching Profession, Not through Their Relationship with Individual Students

The U.S. needs a teaching force that is drastically more diverse to represent the current demographics of the P-12 student population. The disproportionate number of Black students who are suspended, placed in special education, and do not graduate with their cohort suggest problems related to equity and inclusion in U.S. educational systems. One obvious solution to underachievement among Black students is to diversify the teaching force.

After an edict from U.S. Secretary of Education Arne Duncan, the media began to romanticize the idea of having more Black male teachers. We understand that role models are important, and Black male teachers have a strategic position to interact with Black male students five days a week. However, recent media coverage on the lack of Black male teachers has led to many misconceptions and misguided policies. We miss the opportunity to harness Black males' natural affinity toward the teaching profession by promulgating the misconception that Black males are uninterested in teaching. Selection biases within alternative teacher certification programs, such as Teach for America, and documented deficiencies with national teacher certification examinations thwart many Black males' ambitions to teach.

Educational administrators should enforce the policy that every teacher, regardless of race or gender, is prepared to teach any student. White female teachers especially, as the professions' majority, should gain the tools of cultural competence to serve any student regardless of their racial background or gender.

Increasing Black male teachers is important, but as a minority in the teaching profession, Black male teachers should not become props for shortcomings in the educational system. Black male teachers need to be properly trained to meet the needs of all students and all teachers need to be properly trained to teach Black students. It is prudent policy to promote diversity in the teaching force, but irresponsible practice to assign roles and responsibilities based on race.

WHY ARE BLACK MALE TEACHERS IMPORTANT?

Before a school district initiates any efforts to recruit and retain Black male teachers, they should first answer the following questions:

- *What kind of Black male teachers do you want?* Do you want Black male teachers with similar backgrounds, preparation, and perspectives as most of your White teachers? Or are you looking for someone with a diverse background who will challenge existing racially biased views and attitudes at the school?
- *Why do you want more Black male teachers?* Do you want Black male teachers to give relief from students who you don't like teaching? Or do you want Black male teachers as a professional resource to help all teachers (regardless of race or gender), teach all students (regardless of race or gender).
- *What is the role of Black male teachers?* Do you see Black male teachers as overseers and disciplinarians who can keep Black male students in line? Or role models and trailblazers that can help Black male students dream bigger?

- *Why are Black male teachers important?* Do you want Black male teachers to play the role of a surrogate father to "troubled" fatherless Black students? Or play the role of a surrogate school administrator to ineffective and racially-biased schools?

WHEN TEACHERS OF COLOR ARE MISSING, CHECK RACISM FIRST

I was presenting on diversifying the teacher workforce and a White male policymaker interjected:

"At some point, we gotta stop talking about why it's important to have teachers of color and start talking 'specifics.' We need you to give us 'specific' recommendations ... And you're probably not prepared to do that today, but at some point ..."

"No, I can be very specific right now," I interrupted.

"Ask the people in charge of hiring teachers in this district why they aren't hiring teachers of color. That's something specific you can do.

"Usually, when we have these conversations, we assume Black teachers aren't applying. Based on my experience, we have fewer Black teachers because they're not getting hired."

My "specific" recommendation didn't seem to resonate with the policymaker.

Later, a White woman former superintendent at the meeting said, "Dr. Toldson is right, I've seen people not hire Black teacher applicants because their names sounded too Black."

Never, and I do mean NEVER, unconditionally trust the word of ANY employer who attributes lack of diversity to a lack of qualified applicants.

Check racism first.

REFERENCES

Hare, J. (2013). Wanted: More Black male teachers. *Dothan Eagle*. Retrieved from https://www.dothaneagle.com/news/education/article_7ea8b8c2-8134-11e2-be70-0019bb30f31a.html

Harris, T. (2010). Duncan: Black male teachers needed. *CNN*. Retrieved from http://newsroom.blogs.cnn.com/2010/06/21/duncan-black-male-teachers-needed-2/?iref=allsearch

Huntspon, A., & Howell, G. (2012). Black male teachers becoming extinct. *CNN*. Retrieved from http://inamerica.blogs.cnn.com/2012/02/23/black-male-teachers-becoming-extinct/

Lewis, C. W., & Toldson, I. A. (Eds.). (2013). *Black male teachers: Diversifying the United States' teacher workforce*. Bingley: Emerald Group Publishing Limited.

Schott Foundation for Public Education. (2012). *Black lives matter: Schott 50 state report on public education and Black males*. Retrieved from http://blackboysreport.org/

WAITING FOR SUPER-PREDATOR

Why we fear the least violent generation of Black youth in modern history.

***

Being a young Black male is a blessing that people have tried to make a curse. – Demeterious Doctor, 11th grade essayist from the Mile in My Shoes writing competition

During the second 2012 presidential debate, Governor Romney said, "We need moms and dads helping raise kids … gosh, to tell our kids that before they have babies, they ought to think about getting married to someone …" (Follman, 2012). This was in response to a woman who asked about limiting the availability of assault weapons.

In a rare moment of agreement, President Obama responded, "We agree on the importance of parents and the importance of schools, because I do believe that if our young people have opportunity, then they're less likely to engage in these kinds of violent acts" (Follman, 2012).

It was curious how a question about limiting assault weapons inspired moral invectives on single-parent households. In the 1980s, both violent crime and single-parent households among Black youth sharply increased, leaving reasonable suspicions that Black youth were reacting to a more fragile family structure with violence. However, the relationship between the two ceased to exist in the late 1990s, as violent crime among Black youth plummeted, while the percent of Black children living in single-parent households continued to rise. Today, the rate of violence among Black youth is less than it was before 1980, when more than half of Black children were being raised in two-parent households (Toldson, 2012a).

The myth that Black youth violence is rising in tandem with Black single-parent households has more profound implications than the semantics of a presidential debate. The gun industry grew by 158% during the 8 years President Obama was in office, according to Forbes (Miniter, 2016). Invoking xenophobic hysteria, the gun industry conspired with gun lobbyists and gun legislators to make $49.3 billion off of, as filmmaker Michael Moore would say, "stupid White men" (Moore, 2001) who believed Obama was going to revoke the 2nd Amendment.

Since 2008, we have about 46 million more guns circulating in the United States, mostly in the hands of White men who spent billions on very dumb theories. Now, President Trump has inherited a cancer. Since Donald Trump became president, there have been more than 300 mass shootings (Kates, 2017), 1300 accidental shooting deaths of children (Howard, 2017), and more than 60,000 drug overdoses (Tirrell, 2017), mostly from opioid abuse. White communities in the "heartland" of America are starting to look like 1990s Black communities, when pre-gentrified inner cities were reeling from unfettered, government facilitated access to guns and crack.

During that time, Black hip hop artists formed coalitions to make songs like "Self-destruction" and "We're All in the Same Gang." Also, Black mayors and other civic leaders led efforts to get guns off the streets through education, gun buy-back programs, and some of the toughest gun control measures in this nation (Violano et al., 2014). White heartland mayors, Republican members of congress, civic leaders, and country musicians seem unresolved to take similar measures to curb gun violence in White communities.

Wealthy White people care more about billion-dollar profits than they care about White lives. And White politicians care more about contributions from the gun lobby than they care about White suffering. However, the biggest problem for Black students is that White people are ill-equip to honestly confront a White problem without scapegoating. Therefore, White victims of gun violence and opioid addiction can be better assuaged by Trump pointing fingers at crime in "inner cities," than they can by executive or legislative actions to reduce gun (and drug) access to dangerous White people.

After mass shootings committed by White people, White people will hide behind headlines like, "Florida Shooting: Parkland Was Named State's Safest City" (Reilly, 2018) and "Shooter's Mother Had Heart of Gold"[1] (Fantz, 2012). Would the description, "Heart of Gold" be considered if the subject were a Black woman who, like Adam Lanza's mother, was single, collected money without having a job and purchased a cache of weapons, which her son used to kill 20 children?

Notwithstanding the concerning number of mass shootings committed by White people, the typical White response to the incident is to act shocked, blame mental illness, act like these are isolated incidents, and rely on longstanding myths about violence in Black communities for cognitive reprieve.

LAW AND DISORDER IN SCHOOLS FOR BLACK CHILDREN

Police made 2,546 school-based arrests (75 percent Black) between September 2011 and February 2012 in Chicago (Toldson, 2012b). The same year, The U.S. Department of Justice (DOJ) under President Obama filed a lawsuit against Meridian, Mississippi because of their insidious civil violations of Black schoolchildren. In Meridian, schoolchildren were handcuffed, arrested and detained for days for "minor school rule infractions," and without due process (Toldson & Lewis, 2012). Meridian was one of many districts that the DOJ cited for creating a "school-to-prison" pipeline for Black students.

Nationwide, predominately Black, "inner city" schools place a higher premium on security than suburban and rural schools. In 2009, I was on a panel with Ron Huberman who was at the time the Chief Executive Officer of Chicago Public Schools. He spoke candidly about differences in the way that predominately White and predominately Black schools deal with fighting.

He said at predominately White schools, a fight typically results in both students being separated and isolated with an adult, ultimately resulting in a formal mediation process. Contrarily, fights at predominately Black schools often result in both students being arrested by school police officers. It is worth noting that Mr. Huberman is a former police officer.

As I pointed out in my second Breaking Barriers report, nationwide, 26% of Black students report passing through metal detectors when entering school compared with 5.4% of White students (Toldson, 2011). At the same time, Black students are significantly more likely to feel unsafe at their school, and less likely to perceive empathy and respect from their teachers. Many Black students are stuck in educational systems that operate more like a correctional facility and less like an institution of learning. The idea that Black students need to get a "boot in the butt," before receiving a book in the hand, is responsible for many gross injustices committed against Black students in their quest for a quality education.

Unfortunately, many in the Black community tacitly accept the idea that Black children, particularly Black males, are more prone to violence and require tougher safety measures to ensure that criminal elements from their neighborhoods do not corrupt the school environment. However, my research, which I will explain later, clearly demonstrates that establishing a school on a foundation of security has unintended consequences. If Black people are ever to challenge the "school-to-prison pipeline," we must first challenge our own negative perceptions about Black students, their parents, and their communities.

WHY WE SEE YOUNG BLACK AND WHITE
CRIMINALS DIFFERENTLY

On the horizon are tens of thousands of severely morally impoverished juvenile super-predators. They are perfectly capable of committing the most heinous acts of physical violence for the most trivial reasons (for example, a perception of slight disrespect or the accident of being in their path). They fear neither the stigma of arrest nor the pain of imprisonment. They live by the meanest code of the meanest streets, a code that reinforces rather than restrains their violent, hair-trigger mentality. In prison or out, the things that super-predators get by their criminal behavior – sex, drugs, money – are their own immediate rewards. Nothing else matters to them. So for as long as their youthful energies hold out, they will do what comes naturally: murder, rape, rob, assault, burglarize, deal deadly drugs, and get high. (DiLulio, 1995)

John DiLulio is the repentant social scientist who popularized the super-predator nomenclature of the 1990s. He produced trajectory models predicting youth violence would triple by the year 2010. However, youth violence, especially among Black youth, significantly declined. In fact, the declines began before many of DiLulio's suggested reforms were enacted. DiLulio has since acknowledged the flaws in his research methods (Haberman, 2014). However, the inflammatory language he used to describe Black children, under a cloak of research objectivity and the shield of an Ivy League appointment, has longstanding and drastic effects on the education of Black students.

The most violent period for Black youth occurred between 1980 and 1995. Urban violence stemming from emerging international drug markets reached poor Black neighborhoods through a breach in the borders created by President Ronald Reagan's support of the Contras in Nicaragua (Agar, 2003). The Contras funded their subversive activities by selling cocaine to suppliers in the U.S., which was usually sold in rock form to make it more assessable to poor people.

In this post-civil rights period, many neighborhoods and schools across the United States were experiencing re-segregation from "White flight," as critics of forced integration and social safety nets propagandized violence, the crack epidemic, and the rise of single-parent households to chide social reform programs.

Street gangs, emboldened by the unprecedented profits from drug dealing, blemished Black communities. The Crips and Bloods, "gangsta rap," and "the neighborhood dope man" captured the imaginations and influenced the behaviors of socially disaffected Black youth.

At the time, the media was perversely misrepresenting rock cocaine. Rock cocaine received a new name, "crack," which made it appear to be something different from the "freebasing" that White people started decades earlier, and pseudoscience made crack appear to be more addictive and lethal than powder cocaine (Logan, 1999). There was also a heightened level of violence associated with crack in the 1980s and 1990s. However, the draconian drug laws of the 1980s did not address violence, they targeted crack, leading to a surge of nonviolent offenders in the criminal justice system (Patten, 2016).

The juvenile justice systems' disparate treatment of Black and White drug offenders seemed to follow a trend in the way that Black drug crimes and White drug crimes were being depicted in the media and in movies. Contrast two movies of that era, *New Jack City* and *Less than Zero*. In New Jack City, we remember Nino Brown, the drug kingpin of the projects. However, *Less than Zero*'s "Rip," the extremely vile drug kingpin of Beverly Hills, is a vague afterthought. Instead, we remember the poor White teen, Julian, who had to work off a debt to him. *Less than Zero* allows us to see Julian, played by Robert Downey Jr., as a victim, even though he was engaged in criminal activity. "Gangsta Rap," in which Black men pose as drug kingpins who have little or no experience selling drugs, also create powerful images that fuel negative perceptions of Black youth.

Such images create biases and help children who look like a young Robert Downey Jr. appear as victims in the court, while children who look like *The Wire*'s Michael Lee appear as a budding Nino Brown. The numbers demonstrating this bias are stark. According to the National Juvenile Court Data Archive, since 1985, 2,088,607 White juvenile males have been arrested for drug offenses, but only 17 percent have been detained. By contrast since 1985, 958,778 Black juvenile males have been arrested for drug offenses, and 40 percent have been detained.

Black Youth Who Sell Drugs: Separating Myths from Realities

Today, the rate of drug-related arrests is down significantly for Black and White youth, but racial disparities remain. To further explore differences between Black and White youth who sell drugs, I analyzed data from the National Survey on Drug Use and Health (NSDUH) in my second Breaking Barriers report (Toldson, 2011).

Selling drugs might be more common than we expect, however few sell drugs regularly. Of the 5,525 adolescent males who participated in the NSDUH study, 5.6% admitted to selling drugs at least once. Adjusted for the 10–17 male population in the U.S., we can estimate that about 619,745 adolescent males have sold drugs at least once. However, about half of youth who sell drugs, only sell once. The racial breakdown of those who have sold drugs was 6.9% Black, 4.5% Latino, and 4.3% White.

Black youth typically start and stop selling drugs at a younger age than most think. Among the adolescents who sold drugs, most of them were in the 10th and 11th grades, with a substantial drop off in the 12th grade. Black youth were more likely to start selling drugs at a younger age. Almost 20 percent of Black male adolescents who reported selling drugs were in the 5th through 8th grades. Among the youth sampled, a greater percentage of White youth who sold drugs were in high school.

Black youth who sell drugs are poor, but White youth, not so much. Black youth who sell drugs are more than three times more likely to live in poverty than White youth who sell drugs. However, research by Sudhir Venkatesh demonstrated that youth drug dealers actually earn little money, and most sell drugs in the absence of typical youth employment opportunities (Venkatesh, 2008).

Black youth who sell drugs are much less likely to use drugs than White youth who sell drugs. When excluding marijuana, 77% of White, 32% of Black, and 70% of Latinos who have sold drugs reported using drugs. Black youth who sold drugs were also significantly more likely to disapprove of their friends using drugs. White people, in general, are more likely to abuse drugs than Black people (Szalavitz, 2011).

WHEN SCHOOLS BECAME PRISONS

A generation ago, school administrators were scrambling for methods to deal with the looming threat of *"super-predators."* In the early 1990s, criminologists coined the term super-predators to predict a new breed of violent juveniles, who would unleash an unparalleled level of violence throughout the 2000s (Bilchik, 2000). "Super-predators" and "Crack Babies" were 1980s and 1990s tropes that the media used to forecast a conjectural threat from future generations of Black teenagers. Both theories were based on junk science and have since been debunked.

However, Black youth defied predictions, and their violence plummeted in the late 1990s and early 2000s and remains comparably low today.

The crime rate among subsequent generations of Black teenagers did not reach dangerous and unprecedented levels. The crime rate experienced an unprecedented plunge and has now finally reached pre-1980s levels. Similarly, the most comprehensive research studies have found no evidence that prenatal exposure to crack leads to long-term cognitive or emotional impairment, beyond the problems associated with such exposure to any substance including alcohol. Since alcohol is more prevalent, "Alcohol Babies" have always been a more enduring national threat than "Crack Babies."

Criminologists have debated why Black youth violence fell in the mid-1990s. Common theories include the fall of crack prices, the legalization of abortions, and hyper-policing. Nevertheless, public perception of youth violence is opposite the trends. From the late 1980s to present, strategies to reduce school violence is typically based on the assumption that youth violence is precipitously escalating. Notwithstanding, because of the BS about Black children that we were exposed to during the 80s and 90s, and into the 2000s, we tend to expect the worst of Black teenagers today.

Most adults who are in their late-30s and older have been preparing for super-predators for decades. Our confirmation bias prevents us from accepting the fact that teenagers today are less violent and more academically engaged than we were. We see loving, caring, and smart Black teenagers as aberrations and violent Black teenagers as the norm. We also see normal, age-consistent acts of deviance as threatening and tend to respond disproportionately (e.g., a 5-day suspension from school for a scuffle).

One of the most well publicized strategies to deal with school violence came from the 1989 film, "Lean on Me," which chronicled the experiences of Joe Clark. In the movie, Joe Clark rounds up and expels the bad students, and restores order to the school by monitoring the halls with a baseball bat and locking the entrance. Joe Clark's character was based on a real-life principal, who eventually became the head of a juvenile correctional facility.

Years later in 1995, the movie "Dangerous Minds," gave naïve liberals and callous conservatives another peephole into the experience of a real-life change-maker. The movie was based on the autobiography, "My Posse Don't Do Homework," written by a former U.S. Marine who became a high school teacher. Both movies presented a Hollywood caricature of "inner city" high school students and idealized correctional or military-style interventions to deal with "inner city" schools.

The following are concepts that schools borrowed from the criminal justice system (that they need to give back).

- *Zero tolerance* – This controversial strategy makes violating certain laws subject to immediate and harsh penalties, including mandatory minimum prison sentences. Inexplicably, some schools adapted this concept to make certain behaviors subject to immediate suspension or expulsion, regardless of the circumstance.
- *Lockdown* – In correctional settings, lockdown is used to prohibit movement in order to secure a facility, usually in response to a threat. Schools may need to prohibit movement in response to a safety concern, but why call it "lockdown" like the children are in jail?
- *Officers* – Academy trained police officers serve an important purpose in society to protect and serve the population. Correctional officers serve a vital role in prisons and detention centers to secure the facility. The role of police officers in schools is dubious. Ironically correctional officers, who monitor criminals, do not go through police academy training and have no authority to arrest. However, most "school resource officers" who monitor students, complete police academy training and have the power to arrest.
- *Reform* – Criminal justice reform movements have been instrumental in fighting longstanding issues of racial inequities in the criminal justice system. While there are many efforts to improve schools, the use of the term "reform" for schools seems to invite ambiguity. Today, school reform movements typically work in concert with anti-union and school privatization movements. While all schools need improvement, oddly school reform movements focus almost exclusively on public schools' failures and the promise of any alternative to public education.
- *Move* – "Move" is a term used in correctional settings to control the movement of inmates or detainees when large groups have to change locations; for example, to the commissary for meals. In some schools, the movement of students is controlled by using tape on the floor. This happens almost exclusively at predominately Black schools.
- *Metal detectors* – Metal detectors are used in prisons, courts, and other criminal justice settings. In the 1990s, many schools started using metal detectors. After more than 20 years of use, the policies governing the use of metal detectors in school are obtuse and ambiguous. There are schools that have had mass shootings without metal detectors, and schools with no recent incidence of violence with metal detectors. The racial makeup of the school is the greatest predictor of metal detectors' use. About 1 in 4 Black students must pass through metal detectors to go to class, while only 5 percent of White students do (Toldson, 2011).

- *Prison-based labor* – In 2011, then republican presidential candidate, Newt Gingrich, suggested that schools "get rid of unionized janitors" and instead have lower income students perform the janitorial services for the school (Weissmann, 2011).

THE EXISTENTIAL CRISIS OF SCHOOL RESOURCE OFFICERS

In 2017, a White school resource officer, Ben Fields, body-slammed a Black teenaged girl because she disobeyed her teacher in South Carolina. The same week, a Black school resource officer, Thomas Jaha, punched a Black teenaged boy in the face, twice, for not presenting a hall pass in Oklahoma. Both students were arrested. Both incidents were caught on camera. Both officers were subsequently disciplined. Most likely, neither officer would have faced consequences if: (1) the incident wasn't caught on camera; or (2) they would have arrested the children without using force. How many incidents like this occur without being caught on camera? Is arresting a child for being a child just another form of abuse?

Today, school resource officers (SROs) are cancerous to our schools. Many are benign, but they generally place children and adolescents at risk for physical and psychological abuse, as well as premature entry into the criminal justice system. In most districts, SROs go through police academy training and are sworn law enforcement officers. Most of them have stints as traditional police officers. Fields and Jaha are considered "senior" law enforcement officials because of the years they spent on the force. What separates the senior cop who becomes a detective in 10 years, from the one who becomes an SRO? Are senior officers choosing to work at schools, or have schools become de facto "desk duty" for cops who have not performed well in traditional police roles?

State legislators who craft laws that make it illegal to be a typical child intentionally, or unwittingly, provide cover for SROs to psychologically abuse students with unnecessary arrests. For instance, in South Carolina, Section 16-17-420 "Disturbing Schools" makes children who "act in an obnoxious manner" subject to arrest, a fine of up to $1000, and imprisonment up to 90 days.

The hormonal changes that occur during adolescence alone will cause the best child to act obnoxiously. In addition, executive functioning of the frontal lobe is not fully realized until we reach our mid-twenties. In other words, some level of classroom disturbance should be expected, and every school should be able to deal with normal levels of disturbance without arrests.

That's why we require teachers to have a college degree, and administrators to have advanced degrees.

The National Association of School Resource Officers (NASRO) rightfully acknowledges that teachers and administrators should not use SROs to discipline students. However, NASRO should also recognize that their profession is in the midst of an existential crisis. The spirit of SROs as depicted by NASRO is a fantasy. The typical training for SRO is not appropriate for the job duties. Removing bad laws and abuses of the SRO role by school teachers and administrators will not clarify the need for over 45,000 SROs nationally to address the paucity of serious violence at schools.

As professionals, police officers need to divorce themselves from the schools to realize their potential. As a profession, SROs need to divorce themselves from law enforcement to realize its potential.

CREATING MORE OPPORTUNITIES FOR BLACK STUDENTS

"How do we create more opportunities for students to talk to their teachers?" This is a question that a Black male middle school student asked me in front of about 300 of his peers at a school assembly in Little Rock, Arkansas.

A volunteer at the school, who admired my research, invited me to be a guest speaker. I had equal admiration for the volunteer, so I came to the school at his last-minute request. Upon my arrival, the volunteer introduced me to the principal and a teacher who cautioned me about the unruly dispositions of the students. "Most of our students receive free lunch," the teacher stated with a curious degree of consternation.

When the students entered the assembly, I told them, "I'm less interested in talking to you, and more interested in hearing from you. Therefore, I'm going to keep my comments brief and open up the floor to your questions and comments."

After I opened the floor to questions, the slow to warm students quickly began to get involved, asking questions about my experiences as a teen, as well as questions about school life in general. One of the students recited a poem.

Overall, I was impressed by the students' inquiries, as they showed humor, candor, insight, and intelligence. Therefore, I was dumbfounded at the conclusion of the assembly when the principal chastised the students for not asking any questions about Howard University. His parting words to the young men was, "From now on, we're instituting a 'zero tolerance policy' for sagging pants ... so tell your mama if she sends you to school without a belt, we're sending you right back home!"

He completely disregarded the student's meaningful inquiry about student-teacher interactions, instead using the assembly as an opportunity to grandstand, "tough talk," and introduce an ill-conceived zero-tolerance policy. Such principals, who like to summon their inner Joe Clark, are common, well-intentioned and deserve our respect. However, many of their methods to create a secure environment for their students are ineffective and obscure learning priorities at the school.

Such policies are not rare in many predominately Black schools, as the "suspend first, ask questions later" attitude pervades the environment. Questions such as the following are rarely considered: "Why do you sag your pants?" "What might happen to you if you walked through your neighborhood with your pants to your waist?" "What would it take for you to pull your pants up?" Instead of having the type of dialogue to help students understand complicated social nuances, many school leaders in predominately Black schools expect suspensions to do all the heavy lifting.

Over the past decade, I have conducted research that examines the influence of gangs, drugs, and delinquency at school, by analyzing the response patterns of tens of thousands of students who completed surveys for the U.S. Department of Justice and the U.S. Department of Education. From the data, I have gained the following insights into effective strategies for educators, counselors, and school administrators to cultivate an environment to eliminate school violence:

- Elevating academic standards at the school is a strategy for reducing school violence. School administrators should regularly monitor the collective GPA of their schools, and devise strategies to cultivate the academic identity of their students.
- Coping resources and multicultural training should be allocated to teachers who work in tough learning environments. My research suggests that Black males in schools with more gang activity may be more likely to be falsely identified as gang members.
- School administrators who find metal detectors and security officers necessary should examine whether these strategies increase insecurities among teachers and students. The wide racial gap that exists between students who pass through metal detectors when they enter school could be evidence of a larger problem of Black and Latino students being treated

with less deference than White students at school. All security measures should be implemented with compassion and respect.

- School administrators should take specific measures to secure restrooms, secure routes to school, and determine whether any truancy or lack of participation in school activity is connected to threats of violence. My research suggests that school violence typically takes place in locations that are not monitored by teachers, such as restrooms. Also, since students most vulnerable to gang violence are more likely to walk to school, school administrators should build liaisons with the community, and work with surrounding neighbors to reduce violence outside of the school.

- Policies should emphasize the role of extracurricular activities in reducing school violence and improving academic success. Students in schools with less gang activity are more likely to participate in extracurricular activity. Routinely, school administrators should survey students to gauge the overall percent who are participating in spirit groups. Examples are: cheerleading or pep club; performing arts, such as band, orchestra, or drama; and/or academic clubs, such as debate team, honor society, math club, or computer club. If the percentage is low, specific strategies should be implemented to promote school activities.

The Inner City – An Afterthought

I used the phrase "inner city" in quotes throughout this chapter. Of note, "inner city" is an elusive and controversial term, often shortsightedly used to describe a unifying Black or African American experience. In reality, very few Black people live in what most would consider the "inner city." The U.S. Census stopped using the term "central city" and replaced it with "principal city" in 2003. Principal cities are what most would consider "major" cities that have surrounding suburbs.

The percentage of Black people who currently reside within a principal city is 24%, and 25% live in suburban areas; independently incorporated areas within a larger metro area. Another 45% of Black people live in cities, not identified as "principal cities"; most likely mid-small cities that do not comprise the core of a major metro area.

The entire U.S. is becoming more urbanized. Many Black people who live in city cores today have more affluence than some Black people living in what might be considered a suburb. In addition, the migration patterns of White people back into city cores further complicates the notion of the Black "inner city" experience.

So, the whole "inner city" thing is very 1990s, and "sorta wack." We should understand Black people on a deeper level.

NOTE

[1] Notably, CNN subsequently changed the title of the article to "Shooter's Mother Wanted Her Son to Fit In."

REFERENCES

Agar, M. (2003). The story of crack: Towards a theory of illicit drug trends. *Friends Social Research Center and Ethknoworks, 11*(1), 3–29.

Bilchik, S. (2000). *1999 National report series juvenile justice bulletin.* Washington, DC: U.S. Department of Justice.

DiLulio, J. (1995). The coming of the super-predators. *The Weekly Standard.* Retrieved from https://www.weeklystandard.com/john-j-dilulio-jr/the-coming-of-the-super-predators

Fantz, A. (2012). Shooter's mother wanted her son to fit in, friend says. *CNN.* Retrieved from https://www.cnn.com/2012/12/16/us/connecticut-nancy-lanza-profile/index.html

Follman, M. (2012). Romney points finger at single moms on gun violence. *Mother Jones.* Retrieved from https://www.motherjones.com/crime-justice/2012/10/romney-guns-single-moms/

Haberman, C. (2014). When youth violence spurred 'superpredator' fear. *The New York Times.* Retrieved from https://www.nytimes.com/2014/04/07/us/politics/killing-on-bus-recalls-superpredator-threat-of-90s.html

Howard, J. (2017). Guns kill nearly 1,300 US children each year, study says. *CNN.com.* Retrieved from https://www.cnn.com/2017/06/19/health/child-gun-violence-study/index.html

Kates, G. (2017). Report: U.S. averages nearly one mass shooting per day so far in 2017. *CBSNEWS.com.* Retrieved from https://www.cbsnews.com/news/report-u-s-averages-nearly-one-mass-shooting-per-day-so-far-in-2017/

Logan, E. (1999). The wrong race, committing crime, doing drugs, and maladjusted for motherhood: The nation's fury over "crack babies." *Social Justice, 26*(1), 115–138.

Miniter, F. (2016). The gun industry says it has grown 158% since Obama took office. *Forbes.* Retrieved from https://www.forbes.com/sites/frankminiter/2016/04/12/the-gun-industry-says-it-has-grown-158-since-obama-took-office/

Moore, M. (2001). *Stupid White men ... and other sorry excuses for the state of the nation!* New York, NY: Harper.

Patten, D. d. j. p. w. e. (2016). The mass incarceration of nations and the global war on drugs: Comparing the United States' domestic and foreign drug policies. *Social Justice, 43*(1), 85–105.

Reilly, K. (2018). The location of the florida high school shooting was recently named the safest city in the state. *Time Magazine.*

Szalavitz, M. (2011). Study: Whites more likely to abuse drugs than Blacks. *Time.* Retrieved from http://healthland.time.com/2011/11/07/study-whites-more-likely-to-abuse-drugs-than-blacks/

Tirrell, M. (2017). US drug overdose deaths topped 60,000 in 2016, with more potent illicit drug use on the rise. *CNBC.com.* Retrieved from https://www.cnbc.com/2017/10/27/us-drug-overdose-deaths-topped-60000-in-2016.html

Toldson, I. A. (2011). *Breaking barriers 2: Plotting the path away from juvenile detention and toward academic success for school-age African American males.* Washington, DC: Congressional Black Caucus Foundation. Retrieved from http://www.cbcfinc.org/oUploadedFiles/BreakingBarriers2.pdf

Toldson, I. A. (2012a). Insecurity at Black schools: When metal detectors do more harm than good. *Journal of Negro Education, 81*(4), 303–306.

Toldson, I. A. (2012b, November 30). School security boosts student insecurity? *The Root.* Retrieved from http://www.theroot.com/views/school-security-boosts-student-insecurity

Toldson, I. A., & Lewis, C. W. (2012). *Challenge the status Quo: Academic success among school-age African American males.* Washington, DC. Retrieved from http://www.cbcfinc.org/oUploadedFiles/CTSQ.pdf

Venkatesh, S. (2008). *Gang leader for a day: A rogue sociologist takes to the streets.* New York, NY: Penguin Press.

Violano, P., Driscoll, C., Chaudhary, N. K., Schuster, K. M., Davis, K. A., Borer, E., … Hirsh, M. P. (2014). Gun buyback programs: A venue to eliminate unwanted guns in the community. *Journal of Trauma & Acute Care Surgery, 77*, S46–S50. doi:10.1097/TA.0000000000000319

Weissmann, J. (2011). Newt Gingrich thinks school children should work as Janitors. *The Atlantic.* Retrieved from https://www.theatlantic.com/business/archive/2011/11/newt-gingrich-thinks-school-children-should-work-as-janitors/248837/

PART 2

WHY WE BELIEVE

WHY WE BELIEVE

We need to get over the fact that Black boys are brilliant.

***

We need to shift our focus away from why Black boys are failing to why schools are failing Black boys.

This was a message that I posted to Twitter. The message elicited this response from Cato June, a noted a high-school football coach and former professional football player:

Not sure that they are. Kids don't show up. Schools can't fail them if they aren't there.

Coach June's comment ignited a heated debate on Twitter between him, Rhonda Bryant, the author of "Uneven Ground: Examining Systemic Inequities that Block College Preparation for African American Boys" (Bryant, 2013), and me.

Ms. Bryant and I contended that many racial inequities in schools directly result in the missed potential of Black boys to be adequately prepared for college. Specifically, we drew from our analyses of the Civil Rights Data Collection (Toldson & Lewis, 2012), which indicate that high schools with the largest percentage of Black students systematically omit advanced math and science classes, use more punitive disciplinary policies, have higher student-to-counselor ratios, more often have teachers who are not qualified to teach the courses they have been assigned, and more frequently rely on substitute teachers.

Mr. June's central argument was that Black boys needed a system of strict accountability and making "excuses" for their failure is inexcusable. He noted that the school has the responsibility to teach the child, and the child has the responsibility to seek education. Giving a child the inspiration to learn, according to Mr. June, is not the school's responsibility.

He also cited some common themes used to explain underachievement among Black males, including Black boys having disengaged parents

© KONINKLIJKE BRILL NV, LEIDEN, 2019 | DOI:10.1163/9789004397040_010

and prioritizing video games over college readiness. However, the debate ended civilly, with me offering to visit his school in the Anacostia area of Washington, DC, and with him agreeing to invite me to the school.

Mr. June's attitude and beliefs about what Black males need for success and the reasons why they often fail reflect a larger narrative framed from a deficit perspective. Phrases like "crime-ridden," "broken homes," and "drug-infested" are common tropes that contribute to a myriad of deficit-oriented viewpoints that, in effect, condemn the families and communities that are entrusted with shaping the lives of Black male youth.

In order to promote their academic success and well-being, there is a need to delve deeper into the data, as well as go beyond the data, to understand the various ways in which young Black males are surviving, thriving, and demonstrating a level of resilience belied by popular statistics. We also must do a better job of vetting the data to make sure they are true.

WHY WE BELIEVE? FIGHTING FOR EDUCATIONAL EQUITY AND AGAINST STEREOTYPING BLACK MALES

Hello Dr. Toldson: I am the Black male Stanford student who walked up and thanked you for portraying Black males in college as inherently rational. You, unlike many others who study us, assume that our actions have a logical cause. I, and most of my Black male friends, are fueled by altruism and practicality. I appreciated you capturing that. You also showed that, despite rampant assumptions, we have the same lofty aspirations as our white peers. Your presentation struck a chord within me, as I am currently doing my best to become a competitive medical school applicant. You hit the nail on the head when you pointed out that Black males are drawn toward 'helping professions.' My interest in medicine was solidified when I realized I could aid the underserved communities of color I grew up with. – Message from a workshop participant

During a professional development workshop, I showed a video clip of a young Black male describing his feelings of anxiety and despondency when he must pass through metal detectors and encounter teachers that seemed like they "didn't want to be there." A high school administrator who watched the clip shrugged her shoulders and said, "He needs to tell his friends to stop bringing weapons to the school."

In 2013, I participated in a panel discussion with three school-age boys of color at the College Board's Middle States Regional Forum on Education conference in Brooklyn, New York. During the question and answer period, a woman who identified herself as a principal from Maryland asked one of the young male panelists a very peculiar question.

"Why do you believe that is?" she asked.

The young man was confused, and so was I.

In context, the Black male high school student spoke of a "change" that he experienced when he joined the Urban Ambassadors Program in New York. He revealed that the program gave him a new attitude that changed his manner of speech and dress, and motivated him to achieve in school.

The principal, who was a White female, asked the high school student, "How did your friends react to those 'changes'?"

The young man enthusiastically replied, "They love it because they always knew that I had the potential to be something greater, and this program is bringing that out of me."

At that point, the principal scratched her temple, shrugged her shoulders and said, "At my school, the Black students don't like to see other Black students do well, and quite frankly neither do their parents.

"Why do you believe that is?"

The young man's elation dissipated, as his mood began to match her state of perplexity. Innocently, but astutely, he countered, "With all due respect, why do you believe this about your students and parents?"

Her response was as empty as her initial inquiry. Instead of learning a valuable lesson about how to inspire success among boys of color, she came to the session seeking confirmation for her biases. Instead of endorsing the young man as a living testament to the power of transformation through goodwill, she was seeking information to invalidate his success.

All of these negative attitudes about Black students are guided by stereotypes, hyperbole, and conjecture – not a meaningful interpretation of the data and a compassionate understanding of the problem. Worst, these attitudes guide practices that do not address the issues of systemic inequities that exist.

Our school system is replete with administrators and teachers who have biases that are so refractory to change, that they would deny or dismiss living evidence of Black boys' brilliance. The problems with Black boys in schools have nothing to do with Black boys. The problem has everything to do with adults who will believe every bad thing *about* Black boys but unwilling to simply believe *in* Black boys.

The young men who shared the panel with me were cohort members of The NYC Department of Education's Urban Ambassadors program. My involvement in the Urban Ambassadors program stemmed from a book chapter that I wrote in 2009 entitled, "Promoting College Aspirations among School-age Black American Males."

After publication, Rudolfo Ainsley, Executive Director of Programs and Partnerships for NYC Department of Education, used the chapter as the theoretical basis for the NYC Urban Ambassadors Program, which creates college preparatory experiences for boys of color in New York. Several years ago, the program awarded more than $40,000 in scholarships to graduates of the program. Unlike the principal who asked, "Why do you believe?" Mr. Ainsley simply believed.

Among the three students with whom I shared the panel, one of them, Mubarrat Chowdhury, was wearing sunglasses. I am sure many assumed the worst about him wearing glasses, however, he eloquently stated why. After the panel discussion, I asked him to send his philosophy on wearing sunglasses indoors, and he obliged.

In an email to me he wrote:

Whenever I go to important gatherings, peoples' minds are filled with confusion, frustration, and a blend of various emotions. This cyclone of feelings occurs because I wear black shades constantly which in the eyes of many individuals would seem unprofessional, over-the-top, or just plainly arrogant. However, there are elements of symbolism hidden behind this accessory to portray certain aspects of my character. Johnny Cash wrote a song called 'Man in Black,' which spoke about the color black representing the people suffering in the world or the prisoner who's in prison long past his time. Also, I took his words and molded them by just altering the phrase a tiny bit to proclaim, 'I could wear a rainbow and say everything is all right, but I would rather carry a little darkness on my back and show everything else is bright.' The dark meaningful concept was shown by the infamous artist Lupe Fiasco which helped me adopt it and stamp it on my outward appearance to show my internal nature. These glasses also help illustrate the very 'color' of black. It amplifies the idea of having the absence of color, and I wear them to show that I am colorblind for I don't judge people by the color of their skin. I just accept people as human beings. P.S. These glasses are also prescription.

"I am over the fact that Black boys are brilliant," I said during a panel at the Metropolitan Center for Research on Equity and the Transformation of Schools, and the Technical Assistance Center of Disproportionality (TACD) last May at NYU. I said this to about 200 educators, because while I have personally observed countless incidences of young, Black male genius, most people around me appear surprised when young Black males exceed their expectations. At that event, a young man named Chriskapri Smith, an 18-year-old senior at Harlem Renaissance High School, verbally shared his observations of the conference discussions. At the end of the conference, I asked him to email me the notes that he read to us. He wrote:

> There's NO POLITE WAY TO BE RUDE. Marginalized people have been oppressed. Oppressed people have been labeled. When you imagine a marginalized person, think of a box with a label placed on top. Those inside the box, can close it if they internalize the oppression. Those who do not internalize the oppression will try to break free. Will you let them? Will you help? Our society is so judgmental, and full of stereotypes, that most people don't recognize how biased they are. Their biases become a habit that defines who they are. So, if you are trying to help people who have been oppressed, you yourself have to detox biased judgements from your mind. Trying to help someone who has been marginalized when you have biases is like trying to walk in fog with blurry vision. Clear your vision, because you can't lead a person who has been blinded by a box when you are wearing blindfolds. The change begins with yourself. You must be willing to put in time, have perseverance and be resilient to realize your true passion. If you love what you are doing, and respect the people you help, you can do extra because helping no longer feels like work. That's when you're LIVING THE CHANGE. Love the people that you're helping to the point you don't need to be repaid.

If you are surprised that a young Black male, whom I randomly met at a conference, could spontaneously write something so brilliant and profound, you probably do not know them as well as I do. When you truly know young Black males, you expect their brilliance, rather than be surprised by it. We should not repeat the cycle of stereotypes and stigma that led a principal to arrogantly stand before Black brilliance and ask, "Why do you believe?" We need to get over the fact that Black boys are brilliant and use examples like Chriskapri and Mubarrat to justify *why we believe*!

WHY WE BELIEVE – AN AFTERTHOUGHT

A few years ago, I had the pleasure of meeting Barrington Irving. As a child, Barrington believed that his ticket out of the notorious Liberty City area of

Miami was football, until he met a pilot in a convenience store. The African American pilot randomly told Barrington that he should consider aviation as a career, and Barrington's first response was, "How much money do you make?"

Barrington's interests in flying spawned from that chance meeting. He turned down multiple football scholarships to enroll in Florida Memorial University's (HBCU) aviation program. While there, he assembled an airplane, using over $300,000 worth of donated parts, and became the youngest person (not only the youngest Black person) in the world (not just in the U.S.) to complete a solo flight around the world.

Today, Barrington has his own nonprofit that he uses to promote STEM education among school children. In fact, Trayvon Martin's widely known interest in being a pilot was because of Barrington's outreach. At 30-years-old, this brother is just getting started.

REFERENCES

Bryant, R. (2013). *Uneven ground: Examining systemic inequities that block college preparation for African American boys*. Retrieved from http://www.clasp.org/resourcesand-publications/files/Uneven-Ground_FNL_Web.pdf

Toldson, I. A., Braithwaite, R. L., & Rentie, R. (2009). Promoting college aspirations among school-age Black American males. In H. T. Frierson, J. H. Wyche, & W. Pearson (Eds.), *Black American males in higher education: Research, programs, and academe* (pp. 117–138). Bingley: Emerald Group.

Toldson, I. A., & Lewis, C. W. (2012). *Challenge the status quo: Academic success among school-age African American males*. Retrieved from http://www.cbcfinc.org/oUploadedFiles/CTSQ.pdf

BELIEVING IN BLACK PARENTS

Black parents need schools to care more about who they are, and less about who they sleep with.

***

On July 5, 2013, Ivory Kaleb Toldson was born. He is my first son and second child. During his birth, I relived the joy, wonderment, and jitters that I experienced in 2007 when my daughter Makena was born. Like millions of parents, I want the best education for my children. As a Black parent, I am cognizant of the persistent racial inequities and biases in the school system. Black children need to be exposed to a curriculum that builds on their strengths, affirms their culture, and treats them with dignity and compassion.

Notwithstanding many problems schools are having educating Black children, I am optimistic that Black children can succeed in any school type (i.e., public, private or charter) in any environment (i.e., urban, suburban or rural). Through my years of research on academic success, I am convinced that the key to successfully educating Black children is building successful partnerships with Black parents.

Today, the relationship between Black parents and schools is precarious primarily because of antagonists and instigators. Most antagonists speak through a certain movement or organization. Teachers unions, reform movements, and public education advocates can be noble when they focus on children, but destructive when they become antagonistic and defensive. For example, when public schools and teachers' unions defend themselves against criticism, they often use apathetic Black parents and poverty as scapegoats. At the same time, Black parents have become pawns of entities who are only interested in privatizing education in poor communities (while preserving segregated public education in affluent communities) and marginalizing teachers unions. Divisive and ineffective strategies, such as "parent trigger" laws, arresting parents for students' tardiness, and voucher programs, permeate from instigated conflict between parents and schools (Allen & Saultz, 2015; Stitzlein, 2015).

However, the antagonists would not have power if it weren't for a minority of dreadfully negligent parents, racist, classist and classless teachers and school administrators, and policies aimed at berating parents and punishing students. In professional dealings with schools, during my professional dealings with schools, I've heard a White School administrator describe Black parents as "ghetto," witnessed Black parents pass through metal detectors at the school, and routinely heard teachers of all races stigmatize children from single-parent homes. In this chapter, I outline what Black parents should do to promote academic success among their children, and what schools need to do to engage Black parents.

WHAT SCHOOLS NEED FROM BLACK PARENTS

Even though I don't live with my father, he still shows me what it is like to be a man by visiting every other week and keeping his word. It is important for fathers to see their children and teach them right from wrong … It is important for fathers to give their children love and my father shows me how to do this. Young men must have positive males as role models to offer them guidance. (Diontre Miles, 8th Grade, "A Mile in My Shoes" Writing Project African-American Males – Telling Their Own Stories)

Schools need Black parents to participate in their children's education; but without the best data, many schools have difficulty communicating what this means. The implicit messages that many schools give Black parents are that they need to stop being single, turn off the television sets, and help their children with their homework. Based on the data, this advice is shortsighted and elusive.

Research by Hill and Tyson (2009) found three distinct categories of parental involvement that had an impact on children's academic success:

1. academic socialization (i.e., socialization around the goals and purposes of education and strategies for success);
2. school-based involvement (i.e., volunteering at school); and
3. home-based involvement (i.e., helping with homework).

Many are surprised to learn that among the three, "academic socialization" has the strongest relationship with academic success, and "home-based" ranks last (Hill & Tyson, 2009).

When analyzing parenting practices with Health Behaviors in School-age Children (*HBSC*), the strongest parenting indicators of academic success were holistic factors including parents who often told children they were proud of them and parents who let students know when they did a good job. Interestingly, restricting children's behavior, such as time spent with friends or watching TV, did not produce significant effects on grades. In a nutshell, parents who frequently express love and esteem for their children produced better scholars than parents who place a premium on discipline. In addition, parents with higher performing children help their children with school-related problems, are comfortable talking to teachers, encourage their children to do well in school, and maintain high expectations.

WHAT DO BLACK PARENTS NEED FROM SCHOOLS?

Schools should avoid placing unfair and unfounded judgments on race and household configurations. In a research study, Dr. Brianna Lemmons and I found that beyond race and household composition, many socio-demographic variables influence parents' participation in school (Toldson & Lemmons, 2013). Parents who live in urban areas, unsafe neighborhoods, and have young children in the home participate less in school. In addition, parents participate less in school when they have children with learning disorders, speak English as a second language, have low expectations for their child's future, and receive less communication from the school. All of these factors have a stronger statistical relationship to children's academic performance than household composition; however, these factors should not be used to stigmatize parents. Rather, these factors can be used to assess the needs of parents and provide the appropriate school-level resources.

My analysis of the National Household Education Surveys (NHES)-Parent and Family Involvement Survey indicated that schools have distinct ways of communicating with parents across race. Parents of Black children are significantly more likely to receive incidental phone calls from the school, while parents of white children were more likely to receive regular newsletters and memos. Parents of Black children were also significantly more likely to have schools contact them to complain about their child's behavior or academic performance. These patterns create festering tensions with Black parents and reduce their motivation to participate in the school (Toldson & Lemmons, 2013).

In general, parents are more likely to visit the school when they described the environment as supportive. Supportive schools provide:

1. information about how to help children learn at home,
2. information on community services to help their child,

3. explanations of classes in terms of course content and learning goals,
4. information about child development,
5. opportunities for parents to volunteer, and
6. updates on student progress between report cards.

Parents also visit the school more frequently when they are satisfied with the school's standards of academics, teacher quality, and discipline.

BUILDING PARTNERSHIPS BETWEEN BLACK PARENTS AND SCHOOLS

School leaders and parent advocates can implement many culturally responsive strategies to engage Black parents in their children's education. Schools should assess their services and accommodations for parents of diverse backgrounds, including parents who speak a language other than English. In addition, schools should evaluate communication strategies and make every effort to communicate with all groups of parents year-round. Emphasis should be placed on communicating the positive achievements of students and parents. Be creative. Take pictures of parents bringing their children to school and post it on the wall under the banner, "We love our parents."

Instead of stigmatizing parents, schools should broaden their scope and definition of parental involvement to include multiple forms of participation (i.e., school-, home-, and community-based) that accommodate various household compositions and family circumstances. In addition, special accommodations, such as childcare services offered during school events, are an important engagement strategy to consider for these groups. Furthermore, schools should assess their communities for safety issues and engage in partnerships with community members in the surrounding area to promote neighborhood safety and cohesion.

Finally, school leaders and parent advocates should develop strategies to enhance parents' academic orientation. This may be particularly challenging for parents who may have lower levels of education and may not completely understand the value of education to their child's future. However, schools with highly involved parents are resourceful and adept at helping parents to help their children. Strategies to help parents understand the value of education are: Providing college and career fairs, explanations of the importance of specific courses for college admissions and career development, guest speakers, career counseling services, and occupational information.

Together, parents and schools can work together to build a positive learning environment for Black children, if they avoid antagonists who place the needs of special interests and vanity over children. A good relationship between Black parents and schools takes empathy, unconditional positive regard, compassion, and a mutual interest in educating the whole child.

Black Marriage – An Afterthought

Marriage is a personal decision. Social programs that promote healthy marriages to couples or individuals that have already chosen marriage are important. However, social movements that try to socially engineer marriage as a remedy to social ills in the Black community are misguided and dangerous.

Statistically, wealthy people choose marriage more than poor people, but marriage does not make families wealthy. More marriages will not lead to greater levels of prosperity in the Black community. Rather, if Black people had higher levels of prosperity, there would probably be an increase in marriages.

Declining marriage rates in the Black community have nothing to do with a deterioration in cultural values. Declining marriage rates is a natural result of fewer people getting married for the wrong reasons, such as family and social pressure, religion, financial dependence, and protection.

The contribution of declining marriage rates to societal problems, particularly in the Black community, has been grossly overstated and primarily based on BS (Bad Stats). Raising good children has everything to do with how parents parent, not who parents marry.

If you are single, Black, and want to marry, do it for yourself, not the greater good of the Black community.

If you are single, Black, and like being single, your penchant has no bearing on the status or course of the Black community.

If you are a single parent, there are unique social challenges associated with raising a child alone; however, positive parenting and cooperative parenting nullify any statistical relationship between marital status and positive parenting outcomes.

REFERENCES

Allen, A., & Saultz, A. (2015). Parent trigger policies, representation, and the public good. *Theory and Research in Education, 13*(3), 351–359.

Hill, N. B., & Tyson, D. F. (2009). Parental involvement in middle school: A meta-analytic assessment of the strategies that promote achievement. *Developmental Psychology, 45*(3), 740–763. doi:10.1037/a0015362

Stitzlein, S. M. (2015). Improving public schools through the dissent of parents: Opting out of tests, demanding alternative curricula, invoking parent trigger laws, and withdrawing entirely. *Educational Studies: Journal of the American Educational Studies Association, 51*(1), 57–71.

Toldson, I. A., & Lemmons, B. P. (2013). Social demographics, the school environment, and parenting practices associated with parents' participation in schools and academic success among Black, Hispanic, and White students. *Journal of Human Behavior in the Social Environment, 23*(2), 237–255. doi:10.1080/10911359.2013.747407

CHAPTER 12

BELIEVING BLACK STUDENTS ARE COLLEGE BOUND

Black students don't need to know why college is important; they need us to believe they can get there.

***

I had a dream ...

That I published an article about the aspirations of high school students by race and gender, using the High School Longitudinal Study of 2009 (n = 17,587), from the U.S. Department of Education, Institute of Education Sciences, National Center for Education Statistics.

Subsequently, there was a flood of news articles with the headlines, "More than 50 percent of Black male 9th graders want to go to college" or "Black male 9th graders more likely to desire college than White males." The authors of these articles talked about the potential of helping these young men realize their dreams. They also gave commentary on what the Black community needs to do to help the next generation of first-generation college students.

The comment sections were filled with people applauding young Black students who want to do the right thing, while giving meaningful suggestions about how to help Black students who remain ambivalent about their future.

The stat captured the imagination of the public. High school principals in public schools used student assemblies to say to a room full of Black males, "Look to your left, now look to your right ... somebody wants to go to college, and it's my job to make sure you realize that dream ..."

And then I woke up ... but I'll never STOP dreaming.

Most Black Grade-School Students Want to Go to College

Much of the literature on college aspirations among students suggests that Black students aspire to attend college at rates similar to, or higher than, their White peers (Mahoney & Merritt, 1993; Pitre, 2006; Toldson, 2008). In my research, I have analyzed:

© KONINKLIJKE BRILL NV, LEIDEN, 2019 | DOI:10.1163/9789004397040_012

- *Health Behaviors In School-Age Children* found that 62% of Black males (N = 1,133) and 67% of Black females (N = 1,542) "plan" to go to a 4-year college after graduation (United States Department of Health and Human Services, Health Resources and Services Administration, & Maternal and Child Health Bureau, 2008).
- *Monitoring the Future: A Continuing Study of American Youth* found that 45% of Black males (N = 556) and 51% of Black females (N = 581) "expect" to go to a 4-year college after graduation (Johnston, Bachman, O'Malley, & Schulenberg, 2008).
- *High School Longitudinal Survey of 2009* found that 51% of Black males (N = 1,149) and 56% of Black females (N = 1,297) "plan" to go to a 4-year college after graduation (Ingels et al., 2011).

Notably, across all three surveys, the percentage of Black students that aspire to attend college after high school was slightly higher than White students. Therefore, any difference in college participation across races has nothing to do with Black students' attitude or desire, and everything to do with systemic inequities.

The attitude achievement paradox (Mickelson, 1990), a concept described in a previous chapter, is important for developing an accurate perception of the experiences Black students face when pursuing higher education. Many programs aimed at promoting college to Black students operate from a deficit perspective. Fundamentally, they use strategies aimed at teaching "why" college is important, when they should be focused on "how" to get there.

An in-depth look at the data finds that the top reason Black students do not go to college is that they do not think they can afford it. Other factors that limit Black students' progress to college after graduation include: not feeling adequately prepared for college, not having enough information to make the best decision, and competing family obligations. This should change just about everything about how most high schools promote college to Black students. This is also why programs like Urban Prep and Eagle Academy are so vitally important to the Black community.

DEBUNKING THE BS ABOUT BLACK COLLEGE STUDENTS

Black Males Don't Go to College

Black males are not underrepresented in institutions of higher education. Today the 12.7 million Black males, who are 18 years old and older, comprise 5.5 percent of the adult population in the U.S. and the 76.4 million White males comprise 32.7 percent. According to the 2010 Census, the 1.2 million Black male college students comprise 5.5 percent of all college students, while the 5.6 million White male students comprise 27 percent. Purely looking at numbers, Black males are more adequately represented in higher education than White males. There are more women than men in college across all races. Across the 8 Ivy League universities, only 2 have a higher enrollment of men than women. There is also a well-known GPA gap between males and females (U.S. Department of Education's National Center for Education Statistics, 2018).

However, the landscape of higher education is changing for Black males. Distance learning, community colleges, and for-profit colleges are offering Black students cost- and time-efficient alternatives to traditional colleges, yet many questions remain about the quality of education they provide. In 2001, four HBCUs were among the top ten for enrolling Black males. In 2011, no HBCUs were in the top ten and only one (Florida A&M University) was in the top twenty.

The top ten colleges for enrolling Black males are comprised of three for-profit colleges, four community colleges, and three public 4-year institutions. University of Phoenix – Online Campus reported 847 Black male students in 2001 and 21,802 in 2011, making it the nation's top enroller of Black male students. Second to the top is Ashford University, which reported 23 Black males in 2001 and 15,081 in 2011 (U.S. Department of Education's National Center for Education Statistics, 2018).

Today, of the 1.2 million Black males currently enrolled in college, more than 529,000 (43 percent) are attending community colleges, compared to only 11 percent who attend HBCUs. Another 11 percent of Black males attend for-profit universities (U.S. Department of Education's National Center for Education Statistics, 2018).

With respect to Black men, a deeper look at census data reveals an interesting clue. In the United States, among Black people age 25-years and older, 825,414 more Black women have at least a bachelor's degree than Black men. However, in the same age group, 202,381 more Black men have a personal income of more than $75,000 than Black females (Ruggles et al., 2015).

Among Black men who do not have a 4-year college degree, but still make more than $75,000 annually, the top occupations are (1) Truck Drivers; (2) Managers; (3) Police Officers; (4) Security Guards & Gaming Surveillance; and (5) Laborers and Freight, Stock, and Material Movers. However, if "not in labor force" (those making their income through private businesses, investments, inheritance, etc.) was considered an occupation, it would be number two (Ruggles et al., 2015).

In total, 173,450 more Black men than Black women earn more than $75,000 annually without graduating from college. Keeping this in perspective, a Black man with a four-year college degree, on average, makes more than twice annually than Black males who are college dropouts (Ruggles et al., 2015).

Black Students Need a Less Rigorous Education and Less Competitive Options for College

"They're pushing them toward college and they're dropping out … They fall back and don't succeed, whereas if there was a less intensive track, they would," said PA Senator John Eichelberger, who was serving as the chair of Pennsylvania's Senate Education Committee, when discussing "inner city" students. When discussing Eichelberger's comments for PolitiFact, I noted that the senator was proposing the opposite of what Black students need.

Black students do not need less competitive higher education options. Black students need schools that prepare them for more competitive higher education options. Although Black students' representation in higher education is proportional to their representation in the adult population, lack of adequate advisement and academic rigor in high schools have resulted in Black students being underrepresented at competitive universities and overrepresented at community colleges and online universities (see statistics in the previous section). In the current educational environment, even our most gifted Black students with the most dedicated parents can leave high school underprepared. Often, students with very low GPAs, low ACT/SAT scores, and key mathematics and science classes omitted, have difficulty gaining acceptance to traditional 4-year institutions.

I graduated from my state's Flagship University because one teacher in high school cared   I graduated from Istrouma Senior High School, a public high school in Baton Rouge, Louisiana of 750 students, 98 percent Black and 90 percent eligible for free or reduced lunch (GreatSchools, 2012). As a student at Istrouma, one of my friends informed me that Louisiana State University (LSU) required Physics for admission. Physics was not required for me to graduate high school, and I had only marginal interests in attending LSU; however, I decided to enroll in Physics during my senior year because

I did not want to limit my options. My school only offered a half year of Physics (.5 credits), so I was not certain that I met LSU's admissions criteria, but my application was accepted. I enrolled in LSU the summer after I graduated, through a minority bridge program, and graduated four years later.

During my sophomore year of college, I returned to Istrouma to visit my high school Physics teacher; one of my favorite teachers named Mr. Jacob. "Toldson man!" Mr. Jacob, who is White, exclaimed, "I think our principal forgot what color he is." At the time, the principal was Black. Mr. Jacob was upset because the principal had recently succeeded in eliminating Physics from the curriculum at Istrouma High School.

Admittedly, I had the utmost respect for our principal. He oversaw the transformation of the school after we had two shootings and one stabbing resulting in a student's death during my sophomore year of high school. Upon his hiring, he restored order and discipline, but perhaps his myopic view of his responsibilities was not conducive to students like me. If I were born two years later, the man who created a safer learning environment for me might have also denied me the opportunity to attend my state's flagship university.

It's about college prep   Over the past five years, I have spoken frequently to colleagues, teachers, counselors, and school administrators about students who are being systematically denied access to colleges and universities because the curricula of their assigned public school are not compatible with public institutions of higher education. I have conducted trainings with groups of principals and principal trainees who talk candidly about the challenges of providing academic enrichment to students, while meeting social and political pressures to enforce strict disciplinary policies and procedures.

The Department of Education's Civil Rights Data Collection (CRDC) report reveals that problems associated with public high schools under preparing Black students for college is far more pervasive than I imagined. Today, of the 8,550,344 Black children enrolled in kindergarten through 12th grade in the U.S., 95.5 percent attend public schools and 4.5% attend private schools (Institute of Education Sciences & National Center for Education Statistics, 2012). The majority of public school students are assigned to their schools by their respective jurisdiction based on their home address. Therefore, many public school students are systematically denied access to their states' most selective public institutions of higher education because of their address.

The CRDC report, "Revealing New Truths about Our Nation's Schools," reported deep disparities in access to high-level mathematics and science courses in the nation's largest and most diverse school districts, including New York City Public Schools, Los Angeles Unified School District, and Chicago Public Schools (United States Department of Education Office for Civil Rights, 2012). In public schools serving the fewest Latino and African American students, 82 percent offer Algebra II, 66 percent offer Physics and 55 percent offer Calculus. For schools serving the most African American and Hispanic students, 65 percent offer Algebra II, 40 percent offer Physics, and only 29 percent offer Calculus (United States Department of Education Office for Civil Rights, 2012).

In 2012, the Department of Education released the *Civil Rights Data Collection* report. The study suggests that opportunity gaps that exist between Black and White students across the country center around three key areas:

1. Schools routinely offer Black children a less rigorous curriculum that omits classes required for college admission;
2. Schools discipline Black students more harshly by suspending them for behaviors (e.g., tardiness) that rarely result in suspensions among White males; and
3. Black students are the most likely to have the lowest paid teachers with the fewest years of classroom experience, and who become teachers through alternative teacher certification programs.

In a national survey conducted by the U.S. Department of Education, National Center for Education Statistics, 87 percent of Black students who were in the 9th grade in 2009 were in the 11th grade by 2012. In addition, Black students were more likely to advance than fall behind or drop out. About 64 percent of Black high school males expect to eventually graduate from college (Ingels et al., 2011).

However, Black students are behind their peers in the percent who are taking college preparatory classes. Fifty-three percent of Asian students, 24 percent of White students, 16 percent of Hispanic students, and 12 percent of Black students are taking pre-calculus or calculus by the 11th grade.

To increase college participation of Black students, schools need to prioritize aspects of learning and school experiences that are important to colleges. For example, Lamar High School senior, Michael Brown, was accepted to 20 universities, including Harvard, Princeton, Northwestern, Yale, UPenn, Stanford, Georgetown, and Vanderbilt, with a full scholarship to each school (Talarico, 2018).

Lamar High School is a public school located in Houston, TX. It is about 70% Black and Hispanic, and 24% White, and has a GreatSchool.com rating of 5/10 (GreatSchools.org, 2018).

Many high schools prioritize high state test schools when they attempt to improve learning outcomes for students. However, colleges don't use state tests for admissions. Instead of chasing Great School scores, high schools should chase ACT/SAT prep, AP classes, four units of mathematics and science, foreign languages, science fairs, writing workshops, reading agency, STEM clubs, leadership opportunities, and college visits. If we want Black students to be college ready, do, and seek, what matters. And ignore the BS that compels us to simply artificially inflated Great School ratings.

Michael Brown, deservedly, receive considerable media attention for his success. However, we should be cautious about celebrating success to the point of acting surprised. The total population of Black men across the 8 Ivy League universities is 3,385 (U.S. Department of Education's National Center for Education Statistics, 2018). Celebrate the success of the young brothers who get accepted, without acting like a Black man on an Ivy League campus is an anomaly. Expect success.

Black Students' Low ACT/SAT Scores Disqualifies Them from Most Colleges

Throughout the history of the SAT and ACT, Black students' average scores have been the lowest among all race groups. Currently, the national average for Black students on the ACT is 17 (ACT), compared with 22 for white students, and the national average for Black students on the SAT is 860 (Jaschik, 2013), compared with 1,061 for white students.

Black students' scores on the SAT and ACT have been relatively flat for the last 20 years, although significant gains have been made in Black students' graduation rates and college-degree attainment. The disparity in those numbers raises questions about the significance of the SAT in predicting long-term college success for African Americans – or any student, for that matter.

Reasons for lower standardized test scores among Black students have been debated in the academic literature as well as in public discourse. Some question the validity and reliability of the tests, while others assert that the systemic impact of racial oppression and poverty diminishes Black students' performance on the tests.

Other, more extreme explanations purport that Black students' performance is diminished because of natural cognitive deficits or corrupted cultural values. However, as Black families and the Black community have sought to reconcile low test scores, test manufacturers have been grappling with research suggesting that the ACT and SAT do not predict college success.

The National Association for College Admission Counseling released research (Hiss & Franks, 2014) that revealed no significant differences in cumulative GPA or graduation rates between students who submit test scores for college admission and those who opt out of using scores for admission. In addition, the study found that high school GPA correlated highly with college GPA, regardless of SAT or ACT scores. In other words, students with low high school GPAs and high SAT or ACT scores generally performed poorly in college, and students with strong high school GPAs and low SAT or ACT scores generally performed well in college. The total sample of the study was almost 123,000 students across 33 diverse institutions.

Some of the proposed changes to the SAT are aimed at addressing a known achievement gap that could be a proxy for race and/or socioeconomic status – the gap between students who participate in test prep and those who don't. Currently, test-preparation materials began at $25, and test-preparation courses and tutoring cost up to $6,600. More-affluent families spend more money to "train" their children to take the test, which often involves skills that have little to do with crystallizing the knowledge they should have gained in high school. The significant gains in SAT and ACT scores achieved by students who participate in the more expensive test programs, as reported by the test-prep companies, call into question the integrity of the tests.

Whether changes to the SAT will make scores more predictive of college performance and reduce affluent families' ability to "game" the test will not be known until years after changes are implemented. However, the proposed changes will do little to mitigate the widespread use and misuse of the SAT or ACT as an admissions criterion. NACAC's "Statement of Principles of Good Practice" (National Association College Admission Counseling, 2013) explicitly states that universities should "not use minimum test scores as the sole criterion for admission, advising or for the awarding of financial aid."

Today many institutions are liberalizing their use of standardized tests for admissions. Across the landscape of institutions of higher education, the nonuse of standardized tests for admissions appears to be a luxury and liberty of the most selective institutions, such as Harvard and Stanford, which, to be fair, can select high scores without explicitly using a cutoff. The problem, however, is that they can also select low scores (e.g., for legacies, second-language mathematics whizzes, donors' children and athletes) at will because of a socially ascribed status. Elite institutions have the privilege of subjectivity, while other institutions must recoil under a cloak of objectivity.

Because of the serious concerns about the predictive validity of the SAT and ACT, the Black community should not entertain social commentary that links low test scores to any functional impairment of the race. How seriously an individual should take the ACT or SAT has nothing to do with the collective of the race and has everything to do with the individual test taker's goals.

In the current higher education landscape, there are tangible benefits to achieving a high score on the ACT or SAT. However, there are very prestigious universities, high-quality state universities and a broad range of institutions of higher education that routinely accept students who do well in high school but do not have a high SAT or ACT score.

The priority of every Black family and educator should be to teach their children how to study hard and make good grades in school, as well as to advocate for classes and learning experiences that are consistent with a college-preparatory curriculum. Currently, there is an achievement gap for grades (Institute of Education Sciences, 2009). The average graduating high school GPA for Black students is 2.7, and the corresponding GPA for white students is a 3.1. That gap reflects many concerns that need to be addressed (Toldson & Lewis, 2012), but these concerns are often overshadowed by debates about test-score gaps, which become convoluted because of corporate investment in standardized tests.

In addition, any consideration of the gap in SAT and ACT scores or GPAs between Black students and white students should be measured with the same discretion applied to the GPA gap between males and females. This gap has led to a quiet quota system that mostly benefits white males applying to elite institutions that are trying to achieve gender parity (Badger, 2013). Henry Broaddus, admissions dean of the College of William & Mary in Williamsburg, VA, defended the need for admissions policies that accept males with lower GPAs by asserting, "It's not the College of Mary and Mary; it's the College of William and Mary" (Broaddus, 2009). If we offer the same thoughtfulness to students of color as we do to (mostly white) males, one day it can become the College of Hakim, Javier, Mary, Natalia, Nia and William.

WHY WE BELIEVE BLACK STUDENTS ARE COLLEGE BOUND

According to IPEDS, the United States of America has 4,658 Title IV eligible, degree-granting institutions of higher education. Among them,

1,905 are majority minority institutions of higher education (MMIs). In total, more than 11.8 million students are enrolled at MMIs. Here are some of the highest ranked MMIs: New York University, The University of Texas at Austin, University of California-Berkeley, Howard University and Harvard University (yes Harvard is 47% White among undergrads and 42% White among all students). We are rapidly becoming a majority minority country, which is why we need quality education for minorities (U.S. Department of Education's National Center for Education Statistics, 2018).

The school environment plays a vital role in promoting college aspirations among Black students. Specifically, findings from one of my research studies indicated:

- Black students who aspire to go to college have a more positive perception of school, more congenial relationships with their teachers, and perceive school as a safe and drug free environment;
- Black students with no plans after high school were considerably more prone to sense unfairness from teachers and the overall school experience; and
- Compared to white students with no plans, Black students were considerably more likely to feel that the rules and the teachers at school were unfair (Toldson, Braithwaite, & Rentie, 2009).

These school-related findings collectively suggest that Black students are more sensitive to positive and negative aspects of school, when compared to white students. The findings imply that reducing racial discrimination, improving school conditions in disenfranchised communities, and elevating teacher cultural competence are important in promoting college aspirations.

The results reinforce the need for college access programs for Black students. College access programs that emphasize college preparation and funding for higher education could reduce the ambivalence associated with future plans. Programs such as Gaining Early Awareness and Readiness for Undergraduate Programs (GEAR UP) and Upward Bound are US Department of Education programs that support the findings by offering awareness of and access to college for lower income students.

Educational policies would best serve Black students by helping them to develop a concrete plan to plot the pathway to college. Moreover, counselors and teachers should be familiar with issues of racism and justice. An inclusive multicultural curriculum and strength-base pedagogy could increase the sense of belonging that Black students need to cultivate college aspirations.

Research also suggests that teachers are most effective at promoting college aspirations when they have a personal connection with their students. Educational policies should measure holistic teacher qualities including:

- Abilities to make students feel supported and respected;
- Skill at creating forums for students to express themselves; and
- Ability to critique students without making them feel bad about themselves.

Incentives for teachers to become involved with students outside of the classroom, such as through clubs, sports, and other activities, could also cultivate more cordial student-teacher relationships and promote college aspirations.

Dear High School Guidance Counselors,

During a speech, I heard Michelle Obama talk about the anger that she felt when her guidance counselor tried to persuade her not to apply to Princeton. Her counselor told her that Princeton was too competitive for someone with her background. Ms. Obama set out to prove her counselor wrong, and she did.

The story is familiar. A young Hispanic man from Los Angeles told me that his guidance counselor tried to persuade him not to apply to Stanford because his SAT scores were low. He applied anyway, was accepted, graduated, and remained at Stanford for graduate school.

I also watched a documentary called Tale of Two Schools. At a predominately White public high school in Long Island, New York, the guidance counselor told her student that he needed a "reach" school. Only a few miles away at a predominately Black public high school in Long Island, a Black guidance counselor convinced a Black student with a B average that he needed to apply to a "safe" school, i.e., a community college.

These are the points:

- It is not a counselor's job to tell any student what they can't do. It is your job to find out what they want to do and teach them the best strategy to make it happen.
- It is not a counselor's your job to provide a student with the easiest or most convenient option. It is your job to help them to plot the path to the BEST option.

Let 9th graders know that a college will not look at anything they did from K-8, so this is your chance to make it happen.

Let high school seniors know that the only way to guarantee they will not be accepted to a college is by not applying to that college.

REFERENCES

Badger, C. (2013). For White men, affirmative action is a boon not a boondoggle. *The Washington Times*. Retrieved from http://communities.washingtontimes.com/ neighborhood/unstereopolitical-thoughts/2013/jun/25/white-men-affirmative-action-boon-not-boondoggle

Broaddus, H. (2009). Gender and college admissions: William and Mary Dean talks back. *The Washington Post*. Retrieved from http://voices.washingtonpost.com/answer-sheet/gender-and-college-admissions.html

GreatSchools. (2012). *Istrouma senior high school*. Retrieved from http://www.greatschools.org/ louisiana/baton-rouge/389-Istrouma-Senior-High-School/

GreatSchools.org. (2018). *Lamar high school*. Retrieved from https://www.greatschools.org/ texas/houston/3449-Lamar-High-School/

Hiss, W. C., & Franks, V. W. (2014). *Defining promise: Optional standardized testing policies in American college and university admissions*. Retrieved from http://www.nacacnet.org/ research/research-data/nacac-research/Documents/DefiningPromise.pdf

Ingels, S. J., Pratt, D. J., Herget, D. R., Burns, L. J., Dever, J. A., Ottem, R., ... Leinwand, S. (2011). *High School Longitudinal Study of 2009 (HSLS:09). Base-year data file documentation (NCES 2011-328)*. Retrieved from http://nces.ed.gov/pubsearch

Institute of Education Sciences. (2009). *America's high school graduates*. Retrieved from http://nces.ed.gov/nationsreportcard/pdf/studies/2011462.pdf

Institute of Education Sciences & National Center for Education Statistics. (2012). *The Common Core of Data (CCD)*. Retrieved from http://nces.ed.gov/ccd/

Jaschik, S. (2013). Flat SAT scores. *Inside Higher Ed*. Retrieved from http://www.insidehighered.com/news/2013/09/26/sat-scores-are-flat#sthash.u01JdKi8.dpbs

Johnston, L. D., Bachman, J. G., O'Malley, P. M., & Schulenberg, J. (2008). *Monitoring the future: A continuing study of American youth (8th- and 10th-grade surveys)*. Retrieved from https://doi.org/10.3886/ICPSR25422.v2

Mahoney, J. S., & Merritt, S. R. (1993). Educational hope of Black and White high school seniors in Virginia. *Journal of Educational Research, 87*(1), 31.

Mickelson, R. A. (1990). The attitude-achievement paradox among Black adolescents. *Sociology of Education, 63*(1), 44–61. doi:10.2307/2112896

National Association College Admission Counseling. (2013). *Statement of principles of good practices*. Retrieved from http://www.nacacnet.org/about/Governance/Policies/ Documents/SPGP_9_2013.pdf

Pitre, P. E. (2006). College choice: A study of African American and White student aspirations and perceptions related to college attendance. *College Student Journal, 40*(3), 562–574.

Ruggles, S., Sobek, M., Alexander, T., Fitch, C. A., Goeken, R., Hall, P. K., ... Ronnander, C. (2015). *Integrated public use microdata series: Version 4.0* [Machine-readable database]. Minneapolis, MN: Minnesota Population Center.

Talarico, L. (2018). Teen offered full ride to 20 universities, including four Ivy League schools. *USA Today*. Retrieved from https://www.usatoday.com/story/news/nation-now/ 2018/04/05/teen-offered-full-ride-20-universities-including-four-ivy-league-schools/ 490924002/

Toldson, I. A. (2008). *Breaking barriers: Plotting the path to academic success for school-age African-American males.* Washingtion, DC: Congressional Black Caucus Foundation.

Toldson, I. A., Braithwaite, R. L., & Rentie, R. (2009). Promoting college aspirations among school-age Black American males. In H. T. Frierson, W. Pearson, & J. H. Wyche (Eds.), *Black American males in higher education: Participation and parity.* Bingley: Emerald Group Publishing Limited.

Toldson, I. A., & Lewis, C. W. (2012). *Challenge the status quo: Academic success among school-age African American males.* Washington, DC: Congressional Black Caucus Foundation, Inc.

United States Department of Education Office for Civil Rights. (2012). *Revealing new truths about our nation's schools.* Washington, DC: United States Department of Education Office for Civil Rights.

United States Department of Health and Human Services, Health Resources and Services Administration, & Maternal and Child Health Bureau. (2008). *Health behavior in school-aged children, 2001–2002 [United States]* [Computer File] (Vol. ICPSR04372-v2). Ann Arbor, MI: Inter-university Consortium for Political and Social Research [Distributor].

U.S. Department of Education's National Center for Education Statistics. (2018). *The Integrated Postsecondary Education Data System (IPEDS).* Retrieved from https://nces.ed.gov/ipeds/about-ipeds

BELIEVING IN BLACK HISTORY

How to teach Black history without looking like a jerk.

WHO ARE BLACK AMERICANS?

Persons of Black African ancestry live as citizens, foreign nationals, and indigenous populations on every continent as a result of immigration, colonialism, and slave trading. Today, most Black people in the Americas are the progeny of victims of the transatlantic slave trade. From 1619 to 1863, millions of Africans were involuntarily relocated from various regions of West Africa to newly established European colonies in the Americas. Many different African ethnic groups, including the Congo, Yoruba, Wolof, and Ibo, were casualties of the transatlantic slave trade. The Black American population is the aggregate of these groups, consolidated into one race, bound by a common struggle against racial oppression, and distinguished by cultural dualism (Toldson, 1999).

Importantly, the historic legacy of Black people in the Western Hemisphere is not limited to slavery. The Olmec heads found along the Mexican Gulf Coast are evidence of African colonies in the Americas centuries before Columbus arrived in the Caribbean (Van Sertima, 2003). Black people were also responsible for establishing the world's first free Black republic, and only the second independent nation in the Western Hemisphere, with the Haitian Revolution (Geggus, 2001). In the United States, almost 500,000 African Americans were free prior to the Civil War and were immensely instrumental in shaping U.S. policy throughout abolition and beyond. Post-Civil War, African Americans influenced U.S. arts, agriculture, foods, textile, and language, and invented technological necessities such as the traffic light and elevators, and parts necessary to build the automobile and personal computer. All of these contributions were necessary for the U.S. to become a world power by the 20th century.

Racism and oppression are forces that have shaped the experiences and development of Black people worldwide. Although European colonialists initially enslaved Black people because of their agricultural and other expertise and genetic resistance to diseases, they used racist propaganda to justify their inhumane practices. During periods of slavery and the "Scramble for Africa," European institutions used pseudoscience and religion (e.g., the Hamitic myth) to dehumanize Black people (Toldson, 2008). The vestiges of racism and oppression survived centuries after propaganda campaigns ended and influenced all human interactions today.

Currently, racism is perpetuated most profoundly through the educational system (Loewen, 1996). Black students are taught to revere historic figures such as Columbus, who nearly committed genocide against the native population of the Dominican Republic, and Woodrow Wilson, who openly praised the Ku Klux Klan. Although many of these facts are not well known and purposefully disguised in history texts, children often leave traditional elementary and secondary education with the sense that aside from a few isolated figures (e.g., Martin Luther King and Harriet Tubman), Black people had a relatively small role in the development of modern nations (May, Willis, & Loewen, 2003).

Survey data often indicate that African Americans have the highest incidence and mortality of any given mental or physical disorder, are more profoundly impacted by social ills, and generally have the lowest economic standing. While some of the data are accurately presented, rationales are usually baseless, and findings typically lack a sociohistorical context. In addition, studies on African Americans unfairly draw social comparisons to the social groups that historically benefited from their oppression.

Historical distortions accompanying dismal statistics have resulted in many educators and counselors perpetually using a deficit model when working with Black students (Jamison, 2009). The deficit model focuses on problems without exploring sociohistorical factors or institutional procedures. Persons of Black African ancestry have a distinguished history, are immeasurably resilient, and have developed sophisticated coping mechanisms throughout centuries of oppression. Appreciating and celebrating a Black people's legacy, contextualizing problems, and building on strengths instead of focusing on deficits are universally appreciated counseling strategies, which merit greater prudence when working with Black students (Amatea, Smith-Adcock, & Villares, 2006).

DEAR RACISM, I AM NOT MY GRANDPARENTS

"Dear Racism, I am not my grandparents. Sincerely, these hands," reads a T-shirt that has recently become a popular posting on social media. "These hands" is slang for using fists for fighting. Following the controversial election of Donald Trump, and during a time when racists acts have reached unprecedented levels, the T-shirt resonates with many who are motivated to resist racism "by any means necessary."

On the surface, the audacity of the message has shades of the Black Power Movement, when activists like Malcolm X and Stokely Carmichael openly eschewed nonviolent restraint, in favor of self-defense and tactical resistance (Auerbach, 2005). Ironically, the full message of the shirt suggests that the use of "hands" to deal with racism is contrary to the methods used by our "grandparents."

On a personal level, my maternal grandfather, John Henry Scott, spent nights staking out his home and church with a shotgun because racists constantly threaten him and his family for being voting rights activists (Scott & Brown, 2003). Also, my paternal grandfather, Henry Toldson, told a story of arming himself to confront racists who threaten to lynch his son for cursing at a White boy who called him a nigger. Both of my grandfathers were born on plantations and managed to escape the exploitative system of sharecropping.

My stepfather, Imari Obadele, served five years in prison because his organization, the Republic of New Africa, while defending themselves against a COINTELPRO-instigated raid, killed a police officer in Jackson, MS (Obadele, 1998). I also learned, from the book Witness to the Truth, that my great, great grandfather fought in the Civil War in a colored brigade for the Union Army to end slavery.

Importantly, none of my forefathers acted alone; they were a part of larger Black movements with few modern-day equivalents. The original Black Panther Party, Deacons for Defense and Justice, The Republic of New Africa, and The Black Liberation Army are organizations that used self-defense methods that were so advanced and threatening that they led the FBI to start "COINTELPRO–Black Hate" to neutralize and disrupt them (Farnia, 2017).

However, beyond the Black Power Movement, armed resistance has been central to fighting against White supremacy in the Western Hemisphere, from slavery to Jim Crow. The NAACP, which is often mischaracterized as a pacifist organization, spawned self-defense advocates like Robert F. Williams and Dr. Robert B. Hayling. Williams obtained a charter from the National Rifle Association to arm the NAACP and wrote the book, *Negroes with Guns* (Rucker, 2006; Williams, King, & Schleifer, 1962). Dr. Hayling, the founder of the St. Augustine Movement in Florida, famously declared that his men were armed and would not die without shooting back (Henley, 2013).

A white-washing of history causes many to see Black liberation as passive, one-dimensional, and isolated. When we learn about the American Revolution, we do not learn about "Black Patriots" and "Black Loyalist" who fought with opposing views of how to end slavery (Green, 2014). When we learn about the period of slavery, we do not learn about the rapidly expanding maroon colonial settlements of Black people who escaped to sovereign American territories, like the "Negro Fort" in Florida, which engaged in war against the U.S. Government.

We also do not learn about free Black abolitionists who were preparing for armed conflict against slave states in the decades preceding the Civil War. When we learn about the Civil War, we do not learn about the Black men who attacked Harpers Ferry with John Brown, or the colored brigades in the Union Army that were primarily comprised of Black people who escaped slavery (Davis, 2010).

Mainstream education subconsciously and deliberately omits aspects of Black history that make White people feel uneasy, resulting in Black children receiving an uninspiring education that reduces their ancestors to the casual pedestrians of American history. True to the African Proverb, "Until the lion has his historian, the hunter will always be the hero."

HOW TO TEACH ABOUT SLAVERY WITHOUT LOOKING LIKE A JERK

A White teacher in my training in Florida said, "I teach at a mostly Black school and slavery is a sensitive and painful topic ... My Black students seem to feel some type of way about a White woman teaching about slavery."

"How are you teaching slavery?" I asked.

I clarified:

Slavery was more than a 'painful period.' It was a period of active resistance for Black people. From the founding of this nation, when Black loyalists and Black patriots fought on both sides of the American Revolution, to the Civil War, when all Black brigades fought for freedom, Black people fought valiantly for their freedom and actively shaped their own destiny.

Right here in the state of Florida, as a Spanish territory in the early 1800s, enslaved Africans escaped southern slave states to form colonies and cooperative agreements with Native Americans. They even took command of a cache of weapons that the British abandoned after the War of 1812 and defended their "New Land" from invasions and rescued other slaves.

There's documented evidence that, under the command of General Garson, the 'Negro Fort' won several battles, including battles that led to the emancipation of local slaves, decades before the Civil War. The presence of the Negro Fort invoked widespread consternation among southern slave owners. Florida is also the home of many Haitians. In Haiti, enslaved Africans not only won freedom from bondage, but also formed an independent republic through military victory.

Nearby, in South Carolina, Africans escaped enslavement and started sovereign colonies on islands off the coast that predate Plymouth Rock, with African cultural artifacts that have survived to this day. Speaking of South Carolina, it was here that ex-slave Robert Smalls learned to pilot a ship and earned his freedom by commandeering a Confederate warship and delivering it to the Union Army.

Before the Civil War, several hundred enslaved Africans escaped every month and immediately began to shape the Western hemisphere. Some established autonomous maroon colonies, some established roots in other nations, and many joined the abolitionist movements. In fact, when John Brown tipped off the Civil War by attacking Harpers Ferry, he was accompanied by several ex-slaves, including his co-defendant 'Emperor' Shields Green.

Importantly, social and economic inequities between Black and White people are NOT primarily the result of enslavement. Slavery ended in 1865.

BEFORE 1899 we had:

- One governor, P.B.S. Pinchback of Louisiana;
- Two U.S. Senators, Hiram Rhodes Revels and Blanche Bruce of Mississippi;
- More than 20 members of the U.S. House of Representatives; and
- More than 60 state legislators.

BEFORE 1920 we had:

- A Black business district in most major cities, such as Black Wall Street in Tulsa, Sweet Auburn Ave in Atlanta, and Beale Street in Memphis.

Current racial disparities are the result of legal and illegal racially motivated violence, discrimination, and indifference, including race riots, lynching, Jim Crow laws, voter suppression, redlining, segregation, discriminatory hiring, and denial of due process and legal protection.

Therefore, racial inequality does NOT exist because White people instituted slavery. Racial inequality exists because White people never left Black people alone after enslavement ended.

There's so much more to say, but we need to stop teaching about 'slaves' and start teaching about 'Black people' during enslavement.

If you teach your students this, I promise, your Black students won't 'feel some type of way' about a White woman teaching about slavery.

My Response to Kanye West Saying Slavery Was a Choice

ENDING slavery was Black people's CHOICE. Leading up to the Civil War, insurrections and escapes among enslaved Africans were increasing in frequency and intensity. Several hundred Black people escaped slavery each month.

Many of them established autonomous maroon colonies. Large slave refuge colonies controlled territory in Louisiana, Florida, the Carolina's, and Virginia, and were growing in size and influence before the Civil War.

Battles between the U.S. government and Black settlements happened before the Civil War, most notably in Florida. After observing enslaved people defeat their captors and control a nation in nearby Haiti, the U.S. reasonably surmised that ending slavery would be easier than fighting, recapturing, and/or resettling thousands of "new colonist" Africans in southern states.

In addition, in Northern "free" states, instead of forming independent colonies, most escapees joined abolitionist movements. They were able to fortify movements, like the Underground Railroad, which led to more Black people escaping each month. The abolitionist movements also became more radicalized and organized with the presence of Black adherents. John Brown was able to recruit Black abolitionists for his raid Harper's Ferry, which tipped off the Civil War.

Therefore, the Civil War didn't happen to end slavery, as is portrayed in schools.

The Civil War happened because Black people made slavery untenable for the Union.

In America, we don't teach that Britain "gave" the colonies independence. We teach that the colonists fought for it.

We should acknowledge the same for Black emancipation.

WHEN BLACK HISTORY IS A CURRENT AFFAIR

Emmett Till's Murder Is Not a Historical Event

It happened within the lifetime of 17% of all living Americans and within the lifetime of nearly 30% of all living White Americans. It happened during a time when the "Greatest Generation" was young adults and Donald Trump was 9 years old. In perspective, the "Greatest Generation" murdered Emmett Till, and Donald Trump wants to "make America great again."

Emmett Till's murder is not a historical event.

It is a current affair.

This Is America

Medgar Evers was assassinated in 1963. He was 37, and my father was 20.

Evers' murderer, Byron De La Beckwith, was a white supremacist and Klansman who was tried twice in 1964, with both trials ending in hung juries, with all white men on both juries. During the second trial, the former governor of Mississippi, Ross Barnett, interrupted court to shake De La Beckwith's hand while Myrlie Evers, Medgar Evers' widow, was testifying. The taxpayers of Mississippi covered the cost of De La Beckwith's defense through the anti-civil rights Mississippi State Sovereignty Commission.

After the trial, De La Beckwith continued white supremacist activities and bragged about murdering Medgar Evers at KKK rallies. In 1967, he ran for Lieutenant Governor of Mississippi as a Democrat.

In my lifetime, he plotted to assassinate a Jewish activist in New Orleans, for which he only spent three years in prison before being granted parole – Yes, they gave Medger Evers' murderer parole!

While De La Beckwith continued his white supremacist life, Myrlie Evers spent the next 31 years fighting for justice. I was 20 by the time De La Beckwith was brought to justice – he was 73.

As we celebrate Medgar Evers, remember that white supremacy is not American history – This IS America.

REFERENCES

Amatea, E. S., Smith-Adcock, S., & Villares, E. (2006). From family deficit to family strength: Viewing families' contributions to children's learning from a family resilience perspective. *Professional School Counseling, 9*(3), 177–189.

Auerbach, J. S. (2005). Means and ends in the 1960s. *Society, 42*(6), 9–13.

Davis, T. J. (2010). David Ruggles: A radical black abolitionist and the underground railroad in New York City. *Library Journal, 135*(2), 79–81.

Farnia, N. (2017). State repression and the Black panther party: Analyzing Joshua Bloom and Waldo E. Martin's Black against empire. *Journal of African American Studies, 21*(1), 172–179. doi:10.1007/s12111-017-9343-y

Geggus, D. P. (2001). *The impact of the Haitian revolution in the Atlantic world.* Columbia, SC: University of South Carolina.

Green, K. (2014). Black patriots and loyalists: Fighting for emancipation in the war for independence. *Journal of African American History, 99*(1–2), 127–129.

Henley, M. L. (2013). The long civil rights movement in St. Augustine, Florida: Reverend Thomas A. Wright and Florida memorial college, 1954–1963. *History Matters, 10,* 50–74.

Jamison, D. (2009). Returning to the source: An archeology and critical analysis of the intellectual foundations of contemporary Black psychology. *Journal of African American Studies, 13*(3), 348–360. doi:10.1007/s12111-009-9092-7

Loewen, J. W. (1996). *Lies my teacher told me: Everything your American history textbook got wrong* (1st Touchstone ed.). New York, NY: Simon & Schuster.

May, N., Willis, C., & Loewen, J. W. (2003). *We are the people: Voices from the other side of American history.* New York, NY: Thunder's Mouth Press.

Obadele, I. A. (1998). *America, the nation-state* (Scholastic ed.). Baton Rouge, LA: Malcolm Generation.

Rucker, W. (2006). Crusader in exile: Robert F. Williams and the international struggle for Black freedom in America. *Black Scholar, 36*(2–3), 19–34.

Scott, J. H., & Brown, C. S. (2003). *Witness to the truth: My struggle for human rights in Louisiana.* Columbia, SC: University of South Carolina Press.

Toldson, I. A. (1999). Black American. In J. S. Mio, J. E. Trimble, P. Arredondo, H. E. Cheatham, & D. Sue (Eds.), *Key words in multicultural interventions.* Westport, CT: Greenwood.

Toldson, I. A. (2008). Colonialism. In F. Leong (Ed.), *Encyclopedia of counseling* (Vol. 3, pp. 1062–1064). Thousand Oaks, CA: Sage Publications.

Van Sertima, I. (2003). *They came before Columbus: The African presence in ancient America* (Random House trade pbk. ed.). New York, NY: Random House Trade Paperbacks.

Williams, R. F., King, M. L., & Nelson, T. (1962). *Negroes with guns.* New York, NY: Marzana & Munsell.

CHAPTER 14

BELIEVING IN BLACK STUDENTS WITH DISABILITIES

How Black students with disabilities end up in honors classes, while others without disabilities end up in special education.[1]

***

Education is Special

Students who are supposed to be "gifted" get first-rate classrooms with bright motivational and educational posters on the walls, live examples to supplement instruction, current textbooks with colorful illustrations, and teachers with advanced degrees.

Students who are supposed to be "learning challenged" get dilapidated classrooms, no stimulation beyond basic instruction and behavior management, and dated worksheets instead of textbooks.

If a student is already gifted, why do they need extra stuff to support their education?

If a student has learning challenges, why don't we supplement and enrich, instead of compromising, their education? (Toldson, 2014)

Research suggests that Black boys' transition to and through the ninth grade shapes their future odds of graduating from high school (Cooper & Liou, 2007). Today, approximately 258,047 of the 4.1 million ninth graders in the United States are Black males. Among them, about 23,000 are receiving special education services, more than 37,000 are enrolled in honors classes, and for nearly 46,000, a health care professional or school official have told them that they have at least one disability. If Black male ninth graders follow current trends, about half of them will not graduate with their current ninth grade class (Jackson, 2010), and about 20 percent will reach the age of 25 without obtaining a high school diploma or GED (Ruggles et al., 2009).

Black boys are the most likely to receive special education services and the least likely to be enrolled in honors classes. Across Black, White, and

Hispanic males and females, 6.5 percent are receiving special education services, 9.7 percent have an Individualized Education Plan (IEP), and 25 percent are in honors classes. For Black boys, 9 percent are receiving special education services, 14.7 percent have an IEP, and 14.5 percent are enrolled in honors classes. Black boys who are in the ninth grade are more likely to be enrolled in honors classes than to receive special education services (see Table 14.1).

Table 14.1. Percent of Black, Hispanic, and White male and female ninth students with specific school experiences in the United States

	Male			Female			
	Black	Hispanic	White	Black	Hispanic	White	Total
Honors course	14.5%	18.1%	27.1%	22.4%	20.5%	33.3%	25.6%
Repeated a grade	17.9%	13.7%	8.1%	13.7%	7.4%	5.6%	9.2%
Special Education	9.1%	6.9%	8.8%	3.3%	3.8%	5.3%	6.5%
Suspended or expelled	24.7%	13.7%	10.4%	14.5%	6.9%	3.7%	9.8%
IEP[a]	14.7%	11.8%	12.6%	5.5%	6.4%	7.2%	9.7%
Problem behavior[b]	34%	29%	19%	23%	16%	9%	19%
Poor performance[c]	26%	25%	22%	17%	14%	12%	18%

Note: Uses the student base weight. Among questionnaire-capable students (n = 17,587). Source: U.S. Department of Education, Institute of Education Sciences, National Center for Education Statistics. High School Longitudinal Study of 2009 (HSLS:09) Base Year.

[a] Having an Individualized Education Plan

[b] Having the school contact the parent about problem behavior

[c] Having the school contact the parent about poor performance

Having specific disabilities, including learning disabilities, developmental delays, autism, intellectual disabilities, or ADD/ADHD, increases the odds that any child will receive special education services. Among Black male ninth graders who are currently receiving special education services, 84 percent have a disability, and 15.5 percent have never been diagnosed. Among those not receiving special education services, 80 percent have never been indicated for a disability, and 20 percent have. Black males are no more likely to be diagnosed with a disability than White and Hispanic males (see Table 14.2).

Table 14.2. Percent of Black, Hispanic, and White male and female ninth students with specific disabilities in the United States

	Male			Female			
	Black	Hispanic	White	Black	Hispanic	White	Total
Learning Disability	9.0%	9.1%	8.2%	5.1%	5.7%	5.2%	6.9%
Developmental Delay	5.3%	4.0%	4.0%	3.2%	2.1%	2.3%	3.3%
Autism	.9%	.7%	1.4%	.9%	.4%	.3%	.8%
Hearing/Vision	.7%	2.5%	2.5%	.8%	2.4%	1.5%	1.9%
Bone/Joint/Muscle	3.3%	2.8%	1.5%	1.2%	1.9%	2.3%	2.1%
Intellectual Disability	.6%	.3%	.5%	.2%	.2%	.2%	.3%
ADD or ADHD	9.1%	5.9%	13.0%	3.6%	2.0%	5.4%	7.4%

Note: Uses the student base weight. Among questionnaire-capable students (n = 17,587). Question wording: Has a doctor, health care provider, teacher, or school official ever told you that [your 9th grader] has any of the following conditions? SOURCE: U.S. Department of Education, Institute of Education Sciences, National Center for Education Statistics. High School Longitudinal Study of 2009 (HSLS:09) Base Year.

Having a disability is related to other negative consequences, particularly for Black males. Aside from special education, students with disabilities are more likely to (1) repeat a grade, (2) be suspended or expelled from school, (3) have the school contact the parent about problem behavior, and (4) have the school contact the parent about poor performance. When creating a scale which included the four risk factors mentioned, plus special education and having an IEP, Black boys without disabilities were likely to endorse at least one of the six risk indicators, and those with disabilities endorsed between three and four. Using these factors as a reliable predictor of not completing school, we find that students of all races and genders are at least three times more likely to drop out of school than their counterparts without disabilities. Among all races and genders, Black males without disabilities endorsed more risk factors than others without disabilities, and Black males with disabilities endorsed more risk factors than any other group of students (see Figure 14.1).

Nevertheless, the trajectory of Black males with disabilities is not uniformly dismal. Among the nearly 40,000 Black male ninth graders who are currently enrolled in honors courses, 15 percent have been told they had a disability by a health professional or the school at least once. Three

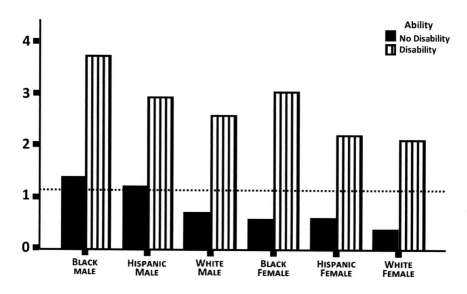

Figure 14.1. Mean number of risk factors for ninth grade students with and without disabilities across race and gender. Note: Scale of measurement is 0 = No specified risk factors – 6 = All specified risk factors. Risk factors measured include (1) repeating a grade, (2) being suspended or expelled from school, (3) having the school contact the parent about problem behavior, (4) having the school contact the parent about poor performance; (5) receiving special education services; and (6) having an IEP Individualized Education Plan (IEP). Uses the student base weight. Among questionnaire-capable students (n = 17,587). Source: U.S. Department of Education, Institute of Education Sciences, National Center for Education Statistics. High School Longitudinal Study of 2009 (HSLS:09) Base Year

percent of Black males in honors courses have been told they have a learning disability; 3 percent autism and 6 percent ADD or ADHD.

HOW BLACK STUDENTS WITH DISABILITIES END UP IN HONORS CLASSES

Having a broader understanding of the true nature of disabilities helps us to have a better understanding of how Black boys with disabilities end up in honors classes. Importantly, a disability does not have to be debilitating. For instance, a learning disorder may be more aptly described an alternative learning style. For some students, mastering an alternative learning style will give them a competitive edge over students who are average "standard" learners. A visual learner could master the art of using pictures to encode lessons in their memory or use "concept mapping" to invigorate mundane text. Similarly, while some easy-to-bore ADD and ADHD students have an irresistible impulse to create the havoc necessary to stimulate their insatiable nervous system, others may use their urges to energize the lessons. They may interject humor and anecdotes or push the teachers to create analogies. While they may have difficulty processing large volumes of dense text, they may be the best at taking discrete concepts and applying them creatively to novel situations.

Every disability has a negative and positive offprint. Most are aware of the social challenges for children with autism that make it difficult for them to communicate with other students or teachers. However, few take the time to understand the advantages of certain peculiar behaviors. In some instances, children with autism can leverage their repetitive behaviors and extraordinary attention to random objects, into the development of mathematic and artistic abilities. Similarly, the scattered attention and hyperactive energy of someone with ADHD helps some children to juggle many tasks, relate to many people, and excel in student activities and student government. Many studies suggest that beyond school, people with symptoms of ADHD often excel in professional roles.

HOW BLACK STUDENTS WITHOUT DISABILITIES END UP IN SPECIAL EDUCATION

According to the Civil Rights Data Collection, of the nearly 50,000 children in DC public schools, 11 percent have been identified as having a disability. Black males account 39 percent of all DC public school students but account for nearly 60 percent of the 5,485 students who have been identified as having a disability, compared with 33 percent for Black females and 1.6 percent for White males.

Interestingly, the percent of Black males with physical disabilities such as hearing or visual impairments is consistent with their representation in the student body; however, they are overrepresented among students diagnosed with psychological and emotional disabilities.

Black males account for 74 percent of students who have been diagnosed with an "emotional disturbance," compared with 24 percent for Black females and 0 percent for White males. White males represent only 4 percent of DC public schools; however, it is revealing that of the 90 White males who have been diagnosed with a disability across 13 disability categories, none have been diagnosed with an "emotional disturbance." Emotional disturbance is the second most frequent diagnosis for Black males across the same 13 disability indicators. The most frequent diagnosis for all students is "specific learning disability."

Importantly, having or not having a disability is not a rigid category. Most, if not all, people have some characteristics of one or more disability. We all have different attention spans, levels of anxiety, susceptibility to distraction, social acuity, etc., which are controlled by past and present circumstances, as well as our unique biochemical makeup. Many Black boys who end up in special education do not have a disability. Rather, they have circumstances that spur behavior patterns that are not compatible with the school environment. Situation specific symptoms will usually remit with basic guidance and structural modifications to the persons' situation. In school settings, from the standpoint of disabilities students can be divided into four categories:

- A true negative – children who do not have a disability and have never been diagnosed
- A true positive – children who have a disability and have been accurately diagnosed
- A false negative – children who have a disability but have never been diagnosed
- A false positive – children who do not have a disability but have been diagnosed with one; *or* have a specific disability and diagnosed with the wrong one.

Many problems are associated with false negative and false positive diagnoses. A child with an undiagnosed disability might experience less compassion and no accommodations for learning or behavioral challenges. A child with a genuine learning disorder might be expected to follow the same pace as other students and be penalized with suspension for opposing an incompatible learning process. False positive children may be relegated to a learning environment that is not stimulating or challenging. There is research evidence that Black males are more likely than other races to have false negative and false positive diagnoses, due to culturally biased assessments, unique styles of expression, and environmental stressors.

WHAT DOES THIS ALL MEAN?

Black males with and without disabilities can excel in schools that have adequate opportunities to learn and a structure that supports personal and emotional growth and development. Contrarily, schools that view disability and emotional adjustment difficulties as enduring pathologies that need to be permanently segregated from "normal" students will stunt academic growth and development. The nearly 5,600 Black male ninth graders with a history of disability who are currently enrolled in honors classes likely benefitted from patient and diligent parents who instilled a sense of agency within them, and a compassionate school that accommodates a diversity of learners. They are also likely to have some protection from adverse environmental conditions, such as community violence, which can compound disability symptoms.

Importantly, Black males are no more likely to be diagnosed with a disability than Hispanic or White males, yet they are more likely than any other race or gender to be suspended, repeat a grade, or be placed in special education. Having a disability increases these dropout risk factors for all students regardless of race and gender; however, the tenuous status of Black males in schools nationally appears to be due to issues beyond ability. One important caveat to consider: some studies suggest that many common drop out risk factors do not predict drop out for Black males with the precision that it does for White males. For instance, frequency of suspensions has a much stronger association with dropping out (Lee, Cornell, Gregory, & Xitao, 2011) and delinquency (Toldson, 2011) for White males than it does for Black males. The more significant implication of this finding is very unsettling; while the act of suspending is reserved for the most deviant White male students, suspensions appear to be interwoven into the normal fabric Black males' school experiences.

While we cannot ignore the injustices in many schools, they should not overshadow the hope and promise of the Black male students who are enrolled in honors classes. In addition, we should respectfully acknowledge schools and teachers who provide quality special education services designed to remediate specific educational challenges with the goal of helping students to reintegrate and fully participate in mainstream classes. Exploring the question, "how Black boys with disabilities end up in honors classes, while others without disabilities end up in special education" may help us to gain a better understanding of an enduring problem, as well as reveal hidden solutions, for optimizing education among school-aged Black males.

I Don't Get it ... – An Afterthought

During a district-wide in-service training comprised of about 200 teachers, school counselors, and school administrators, a man approached me during a break and said, "I'm here to listen to you, not a bunch of

135

side chatter … please tell the room to respectfully keep quiet during the training."

I obliged.

I shared the man's concerns with the group, but I also told them that I get it.

I get that you have multiple ways of receiving information and sometimes when a thought is triggered, you need to expound immediately. Not doing so might feel restrictive and reduce your ability to absorb the information.

I get that you have different attention spans, and while the training has 10 minute breaks after every hour, some of you need to get up and stretch every 15–20 minutes.

I get that you need varying doses of stimulation to maintain attention, which might require anything from a tall cup of coffee to taking a minute to forward a funny picture from your smartphone to a friend.

I get that you have different lives and responsibilities, and some of you come to the training more rested than others. If you appear bored, I will not take personally, and I will not make negative assumptions or judgments about the circumstances that deprived you of a good night's sleep.

I get that some of you might have difficulty sitting in one place for an extended period of time, and you might need to elevate your ability to attend by standing in the back, instead of sitting, especially near the end of a long day.

I get that participating in a daylong training is not an ideal way for you to absorb large volumes of information, and the primary reason the training is constructed as such, is to accommodate my schedule, and to make the trainings more cost effective and logistically convenient for the district.

So, I get this about you, you get this about yourselves, and most of you get this about your coworkers.

But, as educators, why don't you get this about your students?

I don't get it. (Toldson, 2014)

NOTE

[1] Unless otherwise specified, for the data presented in this chapter, the author analyzed 17,587 Black, Hispanic, and White male and female students (Black male N = 1,149) who completed the High School Longitudinal Study of 2009 (Ingels et al., 2011).

REFERENCES

Cooper, R., & Liou, D. D. (2007). The structure and culture of information pathways: Rethinking opportunity to learn in urban high schools during the ninth grade transition. *High School Journal, 91*(1), 43–56.

Ingels, S. J., Pratt, D. J., Herget, D. R., Burns, L. J., Dever, J. A., Ottem, R., ... Leinwand, S. (2011). *High School Longitudinal Study of 2009 (HSLS:09). Base-year data file documentation (NCES 2011-328)*. Retrieved from http://nces.ed.gov/pubsearch

Jackson, J. H. (2010). *Yes we can: The schott 50 state report on public education and Black males*. Cambridge, MA: Schott Foundation for Public Education.

Lee, T., Cornell, D., Gregory, A., & Xitao, F. (2011). High suspension schools and dropout rates for Black and White students. *Education & Treatment of Children (West Virginia University Press), 34*(2), 167–192.

Ruggles, S., Sobek, M., Alexander, T., Fitch, C. A., Goeken, R., Hall, P. K., ... Ronnander, C. (2009). *Integrated public use microdata series: Version 4.0* [Machine-readable database]. Minneapolis, MN: Minnesota Population Center.

Toldson, I. A. (2011). *Breaking barriers 2: Plotting the path away from juvenile detention and toward academic success for school-age African American males*. Washington, DC: Congressional Black Caucus Foundation.

Toldson, I. A. (2014). *In Facebook*. Retrieved December 12, 2018, from https://www.facebook.com/ivory.toldson/posts/10100574421297000

BELIEVING IN FAIR DISCIPLINE
FOR BLACK STUDENTS

We need to lift Black students up, instead of kicking Black students out.

***

In Chicago, an assistant principal told me that the primary reason they suspended students was for coming to school late. He said he just "didn't get it," because no matter how many times they suspended the students, they would keep coming to school late. He asked me if there was anything that he could do about it and my response was, "The first thing you need to do is ask them why they come to school late." His response was, "I never thought of that."

Black students in Chicago are being suspended and arrested at a rate that greatly exceeds their representation in the student body. Several years ago, Voices of Youth in Chicago Education estimated that police made 2,546 school-based arrests (75 percent Black) between September 2011 and February 2012 in Chicago (Harris, 2012).

In Jackson Public Schools, a system that is 97% Black, more students were referred to law enforcement (476) than the number of students who took Calculus (120) or Physics (129) combined in the year 2011. Therefore, in Jackson, MS a student was two times as likely to be arrested than to take a class that prepares them for college.

DISCIPLINE DATA CIVIL RIGHTS DATA COLLECTION

The Civil Rights Data Collection examined disparities in discipline rates between African-American, Hispanic and White students. The report states that while African-American students represent 18 percent of students in the CRDC sample, they represent 35 percent of students suspended once, 46 percent of those suspended more than once, and 39 percent of students expelled. The White students in the sample represented 51 percent of the enrollment and only 29 percent of multiple out of school suspensions. African-American students account for 42 percent of law referrals while in school. Across all districts, African-American students are over 3.5 times more likely to be suspended or expelled than their White peers.

When examining the differences between genders, the CRDC states that male and female students make up nearly 50 percent of the school population, but nearly 3 out of 4 students (74 percent) expelled were male, and males also accounted for 69 percent of multiple out-of-school suspensions. When both gender and race are examined, the sample data state that African-American boys' (20 percent) and girls' (11 percent) suspension rates more than double their White and Hispanic counterparts. One in five African-American boys and more than one in ten African-American girls received an out-of-school suspension. Interestingly, the racial group with the next highest suspension rates among both boys and girls was the American Indian.

Twelve percent (4.7 million) of the students in the CRDC sample had a disability, and nearly 18 percent were African-American males. Students recognized as having disabilities under IDEA were more than twice as likely to receive one or more out-of-school suspensions.

Out of the 20 largest school districts, African-Americans accounted for most students receiving one or more suspensions in all but six districts. African-American and Hispanic students accounted for most suspensions in all 20 districts. The districts with the greatest disparity between African-American enrollment and suspension rates included Chicago Public Schools (45 percent/76 percent), Hillsborough County Public Schools (23 percent/46 percent), Montgomery County Public Schools (23 percent/52 percent), and Charlotte-Mecklenburg Schools (44 percent/75 percent).

The CRDC data also suggest that students with disabilities are more subject to seclusion and restraint than students without disabilities. Students with disabilities (under the IDEA and Section 504 statutes) represent 12 percent of students in the sample, but nearly 70 percent of the students who are physically restrained by adults in their schools. African-American students represent 21 percent of students with disabilities (under the IDEA), but 44 percent of students with disabilities who are subject to mechanical restraint.

ANALYSIS OF WHO GETS SUSPENDED

Let's divide students into two categories:

- Category 1 is comprised of students who have *delinquent behavior patterns*, and routinely bring drugs, alcohol, weapons, and other contraband to the school;

- Category 2 represents students who are *disengaged from school* and routinely come to class late, often miss assignments, and acknowledge finding schoolwork too difficult to understand;
- Category 3 represents students with *aggressive behavior*, who admit to fighting, have taken part in group fights, and have injured others during a fight.

Some might be surprised that Category 2 students are far more likely to be suspended than those in Category 1 or Category 3. Importantly, as a researcher, I did not subjectively create these categories. These categories emerged through statistically analyzing response patterns among the students (Toldson, 2011). Also, there are some students who fit both categories, but not nearly enough to blur their distinction. Many of our most ominous students elude our tough disciplinary approaches, while non-delinquent, disengaged students feel the wrath of uncompromising zero-tolerance policies.

Here are more interesting findings:

- Fifty-nine percent of Black male students reported that they had been suspended or expelled from school, compared to 42 percent of Hispanic males, and 26 percent of White males.
- Females were generally less likely to be suspended from school than males. However, at 43 percent, Black females were more likely to be suspended from school than White males, and about as likely to be suspended as Hispanic males.
- At 41 percent, students attending schools in the South were more than twice as likely to be suspended as students in any other region, including the Northeast, Midwest, and West.

WHY BLACK STUDENTS GET SUSPENDED MORE

Irrespective of race, students who are more likely to get suspended share certain characteristics. At school, students receiving less disciplinary referrals tend to have higher grades, more positive attitudes about school, more school engagement, lower levels of delinquency at school, and less truancy. Beyond school, these students exhibit less hopelessness, more positive self-worth, less thrill-seeking behaviors, less aggression and delinquency, and more parental involvement. When comparing characteristics associated with suspensions between races, Black students report lower grades, more disengagement from school, and more aggressive behaviors.

Black males can become disengaged from school for a variety of reasons including being dissatisfied with school because of noninclusive curricula, racial biases, and poor relationships with teachers. In addition, some Black males are not socialized to the academic environment due to unclear and inconsistent messages about school from home and the community. Finally, some Black males have learning or attentional disabilities that are misunderstood or misdiagnosed.

Based on measured differences between races, it stands to reason that racial differences in the rate of suspensions are primarily due to racial inequities and biases in school disciplinary policies. Other studies have found evidence to support the discipline gap. One study found that Black students with a history of disciplinary referrals were more likely to receive negative perceptions and less deference from teachers.[2] In the *Beyond the Bricks Documentary*, Erick, one of the featured students, testified to his experience of receiving a 10-day suspension for calling a teacher a bad name, only to return to a hostile environment where other teachers "turned on" him.

Elevated public awareness and perceptions of violence have increased schools' reliance on suspensions, zero tolerance and other exclusionary disciplinary policies (Christle, Nelson, & Jolivette, 2004; Skiba & Peterson, 1999). One study found that Black students with a history of disciplinary referrals were more likely to receive negative perceptions and less deference from teachers (Gregory & Thompson, 2010). There are also general concerns about the reliability and subjectivity in disciplinary referrals (Vavrus & Cole, 2002; Wright & Dusek, 1998). Through ethnographic research, Vavrus and Cole (2002) found that many suspensions resulted from a buildup of nonviolent events, where one student often carries the brunt of many students' misbehaviors. However, some studies suggest that school culture and administrative leaders can mitigate high suspension rates (Mukuria, 2002). For example, regular monitoring and analysis of narrative disciplinary referrals have been recommended to improve precision and application of disciplinary measures that are consistent with the students' infractions (Morrison, Peterson, O'Farrell, & Redding, 2004; Sugai, Sprague, Horner, & Walker, 2000).

With respect to disproportionate suspension rates among Black students, many studies have noted the influence of ecological variables beyond the school (Day-Vines & Day-Hairston, 2005). Eitle and Eitle (2004) found that Black students were more likely to be suspended in majority Black grade schools. Cultural expressions of certain behaviors, such as movement and speech, may be misinterpreted as threatening to teachers who lack cultural awareness (Day-Vines & Day-Hairston, 2005). Another study revealed that natural adaptations to life in some impoverished areas indirectly influence the students' chances of being suspended from school (Kirk, 2009).

Improving teacher efficacy and teacher-student dialogue and aligning their mutual understanding of school rules also demonstrated effectiveness (Pas, Bradshaw, Hershfeldt, & Leaf, 2010; Thompson & Webber, 2010). "Whole-school" and schoolwide interventions that focus on schoolwide improvements in instructional methods, positive reinforcement, such as teacher "praise notes" (Nelson, Young, Young, & Cox, 2010), behavioral modeling, and data-based evaluation, have also demonstrated effectiveness (Bohanon et al., 2006; Lassen, Steele, & Sailor, 2006; Luiselli, Putnam, Handler, & Feinberg, 2005). Resilience and skill building among students also reduced behavioral problems and subsequent disciplinary referrals among students (Wyman et al., 2010). Attention to students' mental health may also reduce suspensions and disciplinary referrals among Black male students (Caldwell, Sewell, Parks, & Toldson, 2009).

HOW CAN WE REDUCE SUSPENSIONS?

First, face facts. Students who are slow learners and who lack the wits, social graces, and sophistication to manage learning environments are the ones most vulnerable to suspensions, not students who pose legitimate risks to the security of the school. Giving support tools to disengaged students, such as tutoring, mentoring, and counseling, can reconnect them to the academic process and reduce the odds that they turn to delinquency. Second, we must acknowledge that discipline can become a competing culture at school that alters teachers' perceptions of their responsibilities toward their students.

This certainly does not imply that discipline does not have a role in primary and secondary education. In fact, the third study in *Breaking Barriers 2* (Toldson, 2011) demonstrates that students' grades improve when they can attest to the following: (1) If a school rule is broken, students know what kind of punishment will follow; (2) The school rules are strictly enforced; (3) The punishment for breaking school rules is the same no matter who you are; (4) Everyone knows what the school rules are; and (5) The school rules are fair. This indicates that there is a level of dignity, respect, and order that is necessary when applying discipline at the school. Unfortunately, in many predominately Black schools, students perceive chaos and unfairness in disciplinary policies which create perennial unrest at the school.

Overall safety and fairness of the school influence teachers' empathy and respect for Black students significantly more than for White students, as reported by the students. Black students at unsafe schools also reported more punitive teacher behaviors. Among students of all races, school safety significantly indirectly affected grades, however for Black and Latino students, safety indirectly affected feelings of support.

Critical race theory (CRT) examines White privilege and institutional racism. When viewing a racially diverse classroom with the tenets of CRT, a White teacher who takes a "colorblind" approach to teaching Black and Latino students and ignores social inequalities, inadvertently promotes a racially prejudiced hegemony (Kohli, 2012). With respect to CRT, racial dynamics appear to alter the school environment along racial lines. In one study (Toldson & Ebanks, 2012), White students' response patterns demonstrated a structure whereby teacher empathy and respect were central to students' academic success. School safety had no measurable influence on teachers' compassion for their students and teacher punishment had no measurable impact on students' grades. Contrarily, Black students' response patterns reflected a dynamic whereby school safety significantly diminished the overall level of empathy and respect that students perceived from teachers and punishment from teachers significantly reduced students' grades.

Overall, teachers, administrative leaders, policymakers, grassroots activists, and parents all have roles to play in mitigating high suspension rates among Black students. Congressional Black Caucus (CBC) members, Representative Robert C. "Bobby" Scott and Representative Danny K. Davis, along with Representative Christopher S. Murphy are currently encouraging members of Congress to sign a resolution to improve school climate and student achievement, raise awareness of school "pushout" (suspension), and promote dignity in schools.

However, passing legislation that brings awareness to the high rates of suspension among African-American males will do little to change the problem if people at the local and grassroots levels are not advocating for change and full funding for educational programs. First, we must understand the nature of the problem. Prominent psychologist Abraham Maslow once suggested: "If the only tool you have is a hammer, you treat every problem as if it's a nail." At this point, we need to harness the loose hammers on our school boards, legislative chambers, and schools who are mistaking our Black students for nails, and present sound evidence that these are normal students who have the capacity to achieve in any educational system that prioritizes learning and treats every student with deference and dignity.

REFERENCES

Bohanon, H., Fenning, P., Carney, K. L., Minnis-Kim, M. J., Anderson-Harriss, S., Moroz, K. B., ... Pigott, T. D. (2006). Schoolwide application of positive behavior support in an urban high school. *Journal of Positive Behavior Interventions, 8*(3), 131–145.

Caldwell, L. D., Sewell, A. A., Parks, N., & Toldson, I. A. (2009). Guest editorial: Before the bell rings: Implementing coordinated school health models to influence the academic achievement of African American males. *Journal of Negro Education, 78*(3), 204–215.

Christle, C., Nelson, C. M., & Jolivette, K. (2004). School characteristics related to the use of suspension. *Education & Treatment of Children, 27*(4), 509–526.

Day-Vines, N. L., & Day-Hairston, B. O. (2005). Culturally congruent strategies for addressing the behavioral needs of urban, African American male adolescents. *Professional School Counseling, 8*(3), 236–243.

Gregory, A., & Thompson, A. R. (2010). African American high school students and variability in behavior across classrooms. *Journal of Community Psychology, 38*(3), 386–402.

Harris, R. (2012). Students, CPS spar over school arrests. *Catalyst Chicago*. Retrieved from https://www.chicagoreporter.com/students-cps-spar-over-school-arrests/

Kirk, D. S. (2009). Unraveling the contextual effects on student suspension and juvenile arrest: The independent and interdependent influences of school, neighborhood, and family social controls. *Criminology, 47*(2), 479–520. doi:10.1111/j.1745-9125.2009.00147.x

Kohli, R. (2012). Racial pedagogy of the oppressed: Critical interracial dialogue for teachers of color. *Equity & Excellence in Education, 45*(1), 181–196. doi:10.1080/10665684.2012.644187

Lassen, S. R., Steele, M. M., & Sailor, W. (2006). The relationship of school-wide positive behavior support to academic achievement in an urban middle school. *Psychology in the Schools, 43*(6), 701–712. doi:10.1002/pits.20177

Luiselli, J. K., Putnam, R. F., Handler, M. W., & Feinberg, A. B. (2005). Whole-school positive behaviour support: Effects on student discipline problems and academic performance. *Educational Psychology, 25*(2–3), 183–198. doi:10.1080/0144341042000301265

Morrison, G. M., Peterson, R., O'Farrell, S., & Redding, M. (2004). Using office referral records in school violence research: Possibilities and limitations. *Journal of School Violence, 3*(2–3), 39–61. doi:10.1300/J202v03n02_04

Mukuria, G. (2002). Disciplinary challenges: How do principals address this dilemma? *Urban Education, 37*(3), 432.

Nelson, J. A. P., Young, B. J., Young, E. L., & Cox, G. (2010). Using teacher-written praise notes to promote a positive environment in a middle school. *Preventing School Failure, 54*(2), 119–125.

Pas, E. T., Bradshaw, C. P., Hershfeldt, P. A., & Leaf, P. J. (2010). A multilevel exploration of the influence of teacher efficacy and burnout on response to student problem behavior and school-based service use. *School Psychology Quarterly, 25*(1), 13–27. doi:10.1037/a0018576

Skiba, R., & Peterson, R. (1999). The dark side of zero tolerance. *Phi Delta Kappan, 80*(5), 372.

Sugai, G., Sprague, J. R., Horner, R. H., & Walker, H. M. (2000). Preventing school violence: The use of office discipline referrals to assess and monitor school-wide discipline interventions. *Journal of Emotional & Behavioral Disorders, 8*(2), 94.

Thompson, A. M., & Webber, K. C. (2010). Realigning student and teacher perceptions of school rules: A behavior management strategy for students with challenging behaviors. *Children & Schools, 32*(2), 71–79.

Toldson, I. A. (2011). *Breaking barriers 2: Plotting the path away from juvenile detention and toward academic success for school-age African American males*. Retrieved from http://www.cbcfinc.org/oUploadedFiles/BreakingBarriers2.pdf

Toldson, I. A., & Ebanks, M. (2012). Collateral damage in the classroom: How race and school environment influence teachers' attitudes and behaviors toward their students. *The National Journal of Urban Education & Practice, 6,* 20–40.

Vavrus, F., & Cole, K. (2002). "I didn't do nothin'": The discursive construction of school suspension. *Urban Review, 34*(2), 87–111.

Wright, J. A., & Dusek, J. B. (1998). Compiling school base-rates for disruptive behavior from student disciplinary referral data. *School Psychology Review, 27*(1), 138.

Wyman, P. A., Cross, W., Brown, C. H., Qin, Y., Xin, T., & Eberly, S. (2010). Intervention to strengthen emotional self-regulation in children with emerging mental health problems: Proximal impact on school behavior. *Journal of Abnormal Child Psychology, 38*(5), 707–720. doi:10.1007/s10802-010-9398-x

BELIEVING WHITE TEACHERS CAN TEACH BLACK STUDENTS

Black students don't need White teachers to be better teachers; they need White teachers to be better people.

***

White teachers who teach in predominately Black schools have more in common with their students than they might realize.

They are often compared unfavorably and sometimes unfairly to teachers at more well-funded schools. Researchers use data to paint them as less qualified because they are more likely to be within their first two years of teaching, teach courses that they are not certified to teach, and enter the field through alternative certification programs. While none of this, in and of itself, makes anyone a bad teacher, it can leave White teachers at inner city schools vulnerable to stigma and stereotype threat.

White teachers at predominately Black schools also often have low expectations placed upon them. Unfortunately, sometimes teachers reaffirm these expectations by showing signs of insolence and indifference toward their students. Characterizations of their lack of professionalism have led to some extreme, and often unfair, measures against them; such as attacks on their unions and requiring them to be rated based on standardized tests.

Additionally, like many of their students, people often assume that White teachers who teach at predominately Black schools are there because they have to, not because they want to. People believe that if they had the talent, resources, or connections, they would be at a different school – one with opulent facilities and students with bright blue eyes and private tutors.

But, White teachers at predominately Black "inner city" schools (and Black teachers who have internalized similar experiences) can be excellent and make a difference in the lives of students, no matter what anyone else says.

It does not matter if this school was the first or last choice. What matters is the pride you take in your work once you are there.

© KONINKLIJKE BRILL NV, LEIDEN, 2019 | DOI:10.1163/9789004397040_016

It does not matter if you don't look like your students. What matters is that you treat every student with dignity, respect, genuineness, and unconditional positive regard.

If you have disdain or apathy for your students, their families, or their communities, but continue to stay and collect a check, you are being exploitative and dishonest, and you probably will short-circuit any future you have in education and in life.

The way you feel about your students reflects how you feel about yourself and your career. If you can find and cultivate resilience and optimism in your students, you can certainly do this for yourself and your loved ones.

Remember, at this point in your career, these students are your opportunity to be a more seasoned professional and better person. Never resent them. Even in their immaturity and imperfections, always appreciate them.

If not for them, then for you.

EDUCATION IN BLACK AND WHITE

Several years ago, the media reported that Florida (Toppo, 2012) and Virginia (Deshpande & Noguera, 2012) were attempting to close the "achievement gap" by setting different performance standards for Black and White students. These controversial and misguided proposals demonstrate a dreadfully shortsighted assessment of race and achievement in the United States. Instead of dealing with the complicated racial nuances that shape Black students' classroom experiences, Florida and Virginia are flirting with the idea of "lowering the bar" for Black students, and by association, their teachers.

The 2012 Chicago teachers' strike highlighted the challenges of defining teacher effectiveness in the United States (Liebelson, 2012). Although teaching in Chicago involves significant cross-cultural interactions between teachers and students, racial issues in the classroom were rarely discussed in the media or among school leaders. In Chicago, the preschool through 12th grade student population is only 15 percent White (9 percent in public schools), yet the Chicago teaching force is 53 percent White. Blacks and Hispanics comprise more than 80 percent of Chicago schoolchildren, yet they make up only 40 percent of the teaching force.

In a perfect world, the race of a teacher would matter no more than the race of a plumber. However, research evidence suggests that cultural differences between teachers and students may account for key differences between the schooling experiences of Black and White students (Details on that research follow in the next section). Some school advocates suspect that teachers who lack cultural proficiency may relate to Black and Hispanic students in a manner that undermines their potential.

In many ways, the situation in Chicago is a microcosm of the larger U.S. education landscape, whereby rapid demographic changes appear to be creating fractures in student-teacher relationships and disrupting Black students' learning experience. In this chapter, I consider the evidence that the stark contrast between the race of teachers and students might explain why Black students receive disproportionately harsh discipline, which can result in lower school engagement and diminished academic performance. I also consider the impact of having a majority White and female teaching force in a diverse school system, and whether improving the diversity of the teaching population is the answer.

WHO MAKES UP THE U.S. TEACHING POPULATION?

Teachers do more than just teach content. They stand as models for what it is like to be an educated person. They also serve as surrogate parents, guides and mentors to young people. If students are to believe that they may one day be educated people who can make a positive contribution to society, then they need to see diverse examples. (Dyquan Caldwell, 11th Grade Black male from the Mile in My Shoes Essay Contest)

Today, of the more than 6 million teachers in the United States, nearly 80 percent are White, 9.3 percent are Black, 7.4 percent are Hispanic, 2.3 percent are Asian, and 1.2 percent is another race. Eighty percent of all teachers are female. Relative to the composition of P-12 students in the United States, the current teaching force lacks racial and gender diversity. However, a closer look at the numbers reveals that it may be harder than it sounds to diversify the ranks of teachers, particularly with Black men.

Teachers comprise the largest professional occupation in the United States, accounting for the most professional employees among college-educated White women, Black women, and Black men. Despite the large number of teachers relative to other professions held by college-educated Black men, they represent less than 2 percent of the teaching force, of a student body that is 7 percent Black male.

By comparison, White female teachers comprise 62 percent of the teaching force, of a student body that is 26 percent White female. Considering the entire student body, the United States has one White female teacher for every 15 students and one Black male teacher for every 534 students.

SO, WHAT IF MOST TEACHERS ARE WHITE?

Racial differences between the teacher and student population can matter. In a recent study with my Howard University colleague, Dr. Mercedes Ebanks, we analyzed the response patterns of 8,986 students who completed the National Crime Victimization Survey: School Crime Supplement of 2009. We found that Black students were less likely to perceive empathy and respect from their teachers and more likely to view the school as a punitive learning environment than White students (Sealey-Ruiz, Lewis, & Toldson, 2014; Toldson & Ebanks, 2012).

White students' response patterns demonstrated a structure whereby teacher empathy and respect were central to students' academic success, school safety had no measurable influence on teachers' compassion for their students, and teacher punishment had no measurable impact on students' grades.

On the other hand, Black students' response patterns reflected a dynamic whereby school safety significantly diminished the overall level of empathy and respect that students perceived from teachers, and punishment from teachers significantly reduced students' grades.

These results suggest that many teachers may be operating under an implicit association bias, whereby on a subconscious level, they may view Black children as security risks. Researchers have found that many prejudicial attitudes operate beyond our conscious awareness (Gibson, Rochat, Tone, & Baron, 2017). Nevertheless, they can negatively influence our judgments and behaviors. On the Implicit Association Tests, many people, both White and Black, have difficulty pairing words like "delinquency" with a picture of a White person and "wholesome" with a picture of a Black person. These biases can lead teachers to have dismissive and condescending attitudes toward Black culture because of negative messages they have received about Black people from the media, their families, or their communities.

Working with Black Students Takes Awareness, Knowledge, and Skill

Culturally competent teachers invite open and honest dialogue about race and ethnicity in trainings, supervision and interprofessional dialogue, after confronting their own biases, assumptions, and prejudices about other racial or ethnic groups, and acknowledging White privilege. *White privilege*, or conferred dominance, describes the unearned societal rewards that White people receive based on skin color (McIntosh, 1998), technically, European ethnicity. Unrecognized or poorly understood White privilege can diminish relationships with Black students. According to McIntosh, most White people are unaware of privileges because they are maintained across generations through denial. Neville et al. (2001) posited that White privilege is an insidious and complex network of relationships among individuals, groups, and systems that operate in a racial social hierarchy.

Culturally competent White teachers use professional resources and activities to develop specific skills to accommodate racially and ethnically diverse students (Arredondo, 1999; Helms & Cook, 1999). Sue, Sue, and Sue (2003) described three core multicultural competencies in psychotherapy that apply to cross-cultural teaching:

- *Awareness* holds that teachers are aware of any assumptions, values, and beliefs they may have that could undermine the educational and emotional progress of their students.
- *Knowledge* represents the teacher's understanding of the collective history, experience, and values that underpin their educational alliance with the student. A teacher is culturally competent when he or she can understand how a history of oppression will influence the educational alliance between the teacher and student in cross-cultural educational experiences.
- *Skills* represent the specific techniques a teacher uses to accommodate the unique cultural perspectives of their students (Sue, Sue, & Sue, 2003). Culturally competent teachers use their skills to adapt process-oriented teaching strategies to effectively reach culturally diverse students.

WHITE TEACHERS NEED TO BECOME BETTER WHITE PEOPLE

Racial Identity Development

White teachers who work with Black students need to have a healthy racial identity. In general, White people at lower levels of racial identity tend to lack interest and awareness of other cultures, deny the existence of racism, and often have stereotypes about other races. Contrarily, White people with higher levels of racial identity actively seek accurate information about other races, can perceive overt and institutionalized racism, as well as White privilege, and values cross-cultural experiences.

White racial identity theory distinguishes developmental dispositions of individuals who self-identify as White in relation to their attitudes toward Black people (Helms, 1990). Among them are:

Acceptance: In this stage, a White teacher will accept racist aspects of society as the status quo. They will dismiss or diminish comments or actions that suggest racism exist and believe that Black students need to be more like White students to do better in school. Teachers at this stage are culturally encapsulated. According to Pedersen's five aspects of cultural encapsulation, encapsulated teachers will: (1) define reality with one set of cultural assumptions and stereotypes; (2) be insensitive to cultural variation, and view only one culture as legitimate; (3) have unfounded and unreasoned assumptions about other cultures; (4) overemphasize pedagogical techniques that they apply rigidly across cultures; and (5) interpret behaviors from their own personal reference (Pedersen, 2002).

Resistance: When White teachers are in the stage of acceptance, but are in frequent contact with Black students, they will inevitably be confronted with information and situations that challenge their conventional position. Their natural impulse is to "resist" any information that suggests that racism is real. White teachers in resistance will avoid professional development, try to convince their students that racism is not that bad, and may assert that White people experience racism too. Some White teachers, White women teachers especially, will cry when confronted about racists attitudes or actions to weaponize White victimhood. Interprofessional dialogue among White teachers in "resistance" can be toxic, as they reinforce the worst stereotypes about Black students to justify their underachievement.

Colorblind racism is a form of resistance. Bonilla-Silva (2002) identified the following four major schematic characteristics of colorblind racism: (a) principles of liberalism are extended to racial matters, (b) social and economic racial disparities are explained in societal terms (e.g., dysfunctional family structure, deficient environmental conditions, etc.), (c) racial stratification (e.g., residential and school segregation) is viewed as a naturally occurring phenomena, and (d) racism is asserted to be a thing of the past.

Retreat: When White teachers receive enough compelling information to challenge their beliefs and attitudes about Black students and families, they will stop resisting and may "retreat." Typically, in this stage, a White teacher will be hypersensitive to racism and feel sorry for their Black students. Notably, simply feeling sorry for Black students does not provide the awareness and compassion necessary to adequately nurture Black students. The fragility of White people's ego at this stage may make them vulnerable to tense interactions with Black and White people that could leave them confused and cause them to revert to resistance.

Emergence and Integrative Awareness: As White teachers gain more insight and awareness of complex social issues, they develop a healthier perception of race. They replace feelings of pity and shame with advanced understandings of hope and resilience among people of color. They use cross-cultural exchanges as opportunities to learn and are more sophisticated in their exchanges with White people who are not culturally aware. They understand White privilege, and are neither embarrassed by it, nor accept it as the status quo. They believe in their ability to make a positive difference in society, and advance racial harmony. White teachers who have emerged do not believe BS about Black students or their families. When working to resolve an "achievement gap," they can help Black students on an individual level, while using their social capital to also scrutinize social racism. They use humanistic approaches including empathy, unconditional positive regard, and altruism to not only "teach" Black students, but also to "reach" them.

BEYOND BLACK AND WHITE

This has negative effects on both ends, as teachers formulate stereotypes about Black male students, and these students fight less to battle those stereotypes. The result is the academic failure of Black male students who feel as though the school system failed them long before they gave up on the system. (White Female Teacher challenging BS)

Any teacher, regardless of race, ethnicity, or gender, can teach Black students. Recent media coverage on the lack of Black male teachers has led to many misconceptions. The growing practice of assigning students to classes based on the race of the teacher is both unethical and misinformed. Increasing the presence of Black male teachers improves the diversity of the profession and should be viewed as a benefit to the system, as they provide quality services to all students regardless of race or gender. However, many people falsely believe that Black male teachers have a primary responsibility to foster the social development of Black male students. Black male teachers should not become a prop for failed educational and economic policies.

On the issue of setting different performance standards by race, Asians outperfom Whites on most, if not all, achievement tests. This well-known fact is not viewed as a deficiency among white students. But beyond race, to set fair standards based on backgrounds, we would need to separate Cambodians and Filipinos from the rest of Asians, because most indicators suggest that they underperform Blacks. We would also need to separate Nigerians and Ghanaians from the rest of Blacks, because most indicators suggest that they outperform Whites. We should also separate poor Whites from more affluent Whites – Or, we can simply stop betting our educational future on tests and use more legitimate measures of academic progress. Additionally, teacher performance should not be based on test scores.

Cultivating Happiness vs. Fetishizing Grit

I sat next to a middle-age White woman who was an educational researcher from Portland, OR at a dinner. After learning about my work, she told me that she was working with a school that was having "challenges with Black males." I asked many questions. "What type of school is it?" "What are the demographics?" "What learning approach are they using?" "How are the Black males doing compared to Black females at the school?"

After listening to her describe the school, this was my response:

> Based on what I've heard, I'm not convinced that the school has a Black male problem. I've never seen a similar system work for White males. I've never seen a school that requires White males to puff their cheeks and place a finger over their lips or walk through lines formed from tape from one class to the next. I've never seen a White student adapt to zero tolerance, military style learning drills, or have to 'earn' their desk. Until I see it attempted with and working for White males, I have no objective evidence that Black males are the problem at this type of school.

She pondered my reply for a moment before pointedly stating, "My son would curse out every teacher at the school if they tried that with him."

Profoundly, she tacitly admitted endorsing the fiction that certain educational systems are exclusively designed for my Black son, and if my son does not adapt, something is wrong with him. But to her son's defiance, all she can offer is coy indifference – an indifference not earned, but socially ascribed through racial hegemony.

In my Breaking Barriers (Toldson, 2008) reports, I analyzed Health Behaviors in School-age Children (HBSC) and found that academically successful Black males were almost twice as likely to report feeling "happy" about their life when compared to those with failing grades. I also analyzed the NCVS: School Crime Supplement (NCVS-SCS) and found that Black male students who were successful perceived their teachers to be respectful people who treated them like they matter and nurturers who build up their strengths, instead of making them "feel bad" about their weaknesses.

There is a mountain of empirical evidence that happy learners are the best learners. However, many schools, and some parents, have sadistic fantasies about beating Black students into submission. They grab a bat and harness their inner Joe Clark, binge on memories of "scared straight," and design programs that beat students down, rather than lift them up.

They cut programs, like sports and music, that bring students joy, and double up on test prep. And if students fail, they blame it on their lack of "grit" and not on their healthy intolerance for crap. Black students need educational leaders to cultivate happiness in schools; not fetishize about them "gritting" through their oppressive programs.

All of this brings to mind Asa Fludd, a Black male 11th grader whom I quoted in Breaking Barriers: Plotting the Path to Academic Success for School-age African American Males (Toldson, 2008). He said:

> It was at school where I met teachers who are concerned about my education. One of those teachers is my AP US History teacher, Melissa Soule. Besides making history an exciting class, Ms. Soule expressed the realities of minorities living in the United States, especially Black men. She made me realize that struggle can be a luxury when you achieve because it makes you the person who you are. Besides Ms. Soule, there are other teachers who influence me to do my best, many of them being Black men.

For Black male students like Asa, Black male teachers who serve as models are a luxury, but committed teachers who respect and care about them as a person are a necessity.

The Problem with School – An Afterthought

The basic units of school-based education are teachers talking and learners listening. But some teachers don't talk well. They're boring, awkward, condescending, unwitty, offensive, and/or uninspiring. And some students don't listen well. They are restless, distractible, impulsive, imaginative, and/or have short attention spans.

Good learning in school isn't facilitated by the most knowledgeable teachers teaching the smartest students; learning is facilitated by the best talkers talking to the best listeners. Therefore, students who are good talkers are often perceived as disobedient, especially if they aren't good listeners.

And teachers who are good listeners are often perceived as inept, especially if they aren't good talkers.

But the real problem is not bad teachers and bad students. The problem is a school system that believes the best way to facilitate learning is to transmit static instruction to passive learners.

The problem is a system that has not meaningfully evolved since the agricultural age – a system with a calendar based on harvest bloom and two-parent, single-income homes.

The problem is a system that has not fully integrated any learning devices, beyond human speech, into the classrooms, since the universal adoption of text books and visual aids – a system that treats labs and field trips as nonessential indulgences.

We need to evolve schools into a fully interactive learning environment, where good teachers are masters of facilitating novel learning experiences, and good students are open to new experiences.

REFERENCES

Arredondo, P. (1999). Multicultural counseling competencies as tools to address oppression and racism. *Journal of Counseling and Development, 77*, 102–108.

Bonilla-Silva, E. (2002). The linguistics of color blind racism: How to talk nasty about Blacks without sounding 'racist.' *Critical Sociology, 28*(1–2), 41.

Deshpande, A., & Noguera, P. (2012). Dubiously closing the achievement gap: The Virginia department of education has essentially institutionalized low expectations. *The Huffington Post.* Retrieved from https://www.huffingtonpost.com/anjali-deshpande/virginia-achievement-gap_b_1874722.html

Gibson, B. L., Rochat, P., Tone, E. B., & Baron, A. S. (2017). Sources of implicit and explicit intergroup race bias among African-American children and young adults. *PLoS ONE, 12*(9), 1–18. doi:10.1371/journal.pone.0183015

Helms, J. E. (1990). *Black and White racial identity: Theory, research, and practice.* Westport, CN: Greenwood Press.

Helms, J. E., & Cook, D. A. (1999). *Using race and culture in counseling and psychotherapy: Theory and process.* Needham Heights, MA: Allyn & Bacon.

Liebelson, D. (2012). What happened with the Chicago teacher strike, explained. *Mother Jones.* Retrieved from https://www.motherjones.com/politics/2012/09/teachers-strike-chicago-explained/

McIntosh, P. (1998). White privilege: Unpacking the invisible knapsack. In M. McGoldrick (Ed.), *Re-visioning family therapy: Race, culture, and gender in clinical practice* (pp. 147–152). New York, NY: Guilford.

Pedersen, P. (2002). *Counseling across cultures* (5th ed.). Thousand Oaks, CA: Sage Publications.

Sealey-Ruiz, Y., Lewis, C. W., & Toldson, I. A. (Eds.). (2014). *Teacher education and Black communities: Implications for access, equity and achievement.* Charlotte, NC: Information Age Publishing.

Sue, D. W., & Sue, D. (2003). *Counseling the culturally diverse: Theory and practice* (4th ed.). New York, NY: J. Wiley.

Toldson, I. A. (2008). *Breaking barriers: Plotting the path to academic success for school-age African American males.* Washington, DC: Congressional Black Caucus Foundation.

Toldson, I. A., & Ebanks, M. E. (2012). Collateral damage in the classroom: How race and school environment influence teachers' attitudes and behaviors toward their students. *The National Journal of Urban Education & Practice, 6*(1), 20–40.

Toppo, G. (2012). Florida schools' race-based plan draws criticism. *USA Today.* Retrieved from https://www.usatoday.com/story/news/nation/2012/10/11/florida-schools-race-based-goals/1626723/

BELIEVING IN BLACK COLLEGES

What Justice Scalia, and others, got wrong about Historically Black Colleges and University.

***

Supreme Court Justice Antonin Scalia passed away on February 13, 2016, only two months after arguing against affirmative action because, according to him, Black students are better-suited for "a less-advanced school, a slower-track school." Based on the graduation rates, there is no support for Justice Scalia's claim that the nation's highest ranked institutions are "too fast" for Black students. In fact, the opposite is true. Black students have the lowest graduation rates at non-competitive community colleges and for-profit colleges and the highest graduation rates at more selective institutions, irrespective of affirmative action policies.

According to The Integrated Postsecondary Education Data System (IPEDS) the three universities that have the highest graduation rates for Black students are Yale (98 percent), Harvard (97 percent) and Princeton (97 percent). Stanford University, a private university with an affirmative action policy, has a 91 percent graduation rate for Black students; yet the University of California-Berkeley, a state university that follows a state-wide ban on affirmative action, has a 77 percent graduation rate for Black students (National Center for Education Statistics, 2015).

However, there is partial truth to Justice Scalia's point that, "most of the Black scientists in this country don't come from schools like the University of Texas." According to data from the National Science Foundation, Black scientists are most likely to come from two basic types of institutions: (a) institutions with a Carnegie classification of "Very High Research Activity," and (b) HBCUs (Fiegener & Proudfoot, 2013).

According to a recent report from the National Science Foundation, 21 of the top 50 institutions for producing Black graduates who go on to receive their doctorates in Science and Engineering (S&E) are HBCUs. Among the 29 traditionally White institutions (TWIs), all but four have a Carnegie

© KONINKLIJKE BRILL NV, LEIDEN, 2019 | DOI:10.1163/9789004397040_017

classification of "Very High Research Activity" (Fiegener & Proudfoot, 2013).

HBCUs produce Black scientists because they don't focus on weeding out students; they focus on building up students. Among the HBCUs, none have a Carnegie classification of "Very High Research Activity," and only two have a classification of "High." In total, among the top 50 institutions, HBCUs collectively produced 1,819 Black graduates who earned a doctorate in S&E, TWIs produced 1,600, and foreign institutions produced 798 (Fiegener & Proudfoot, 2013).

None of the southern TWIs, such as Georgia State University (GSU), University of Southern Mississippi, and University of Memphis, which are known to have a Black enrollment that is larger than most single HBCUs, made the top 50. With more than 10,000 Black students, GSU enrolls more Black students than the entire Atlanta University Consortium (AUC) combined, yet every AUC school (Clark, Morehouse, and Spelman) made the list, but GSU did not.

When it comes to producing Black graduates who go on to earn PhDs, HBCUs compete successfully with the nation's best universities, including Ivy League universities, elite private colleges, and flagship state universities. There really is no comparison between HBCUs and non-research intensive TWIs.

Are HBCUs more successful in producing Black scientists because they are "slower-track?" The answer is no.

I spoke at a Black History Month event for one of the largest aircraft manufacturers in the nation. At a private dinner with executives of the company, someone spoke of the difficulties with recruiting Black engineers to the company. He believed that the difficulty of STEM majors in college reduced the pool of potential applicants.

This was my response:

> You can make any major as easy or as difficult as you want it to be. In theory, philosophy could be the most difficult major at the university, and engineering could be the easiest, depending on how the classes are structured and taught. STEM disciplines are not difficult by nature; they are difficult by design. Because they are popular, specific courses are included in the curriculum to 'weed out' students. However, the difficult aspects of these courses have nothing to do with the ability or potential to build your product.

Interestingly, no one challenged my audacity to assert that 'weed out' courses did not build any skills associated with producing aircraft.

HBCU undergraduate classes are often structured more like TWI graduate courses; in that the coursework is more diverse, professors are more understanding, and the overall goal is to teach for a better understanding, not eliminate the perceived weak. Furthermore, most HBCU graduates receive their PhD in STEM disciplines from TWIs; further demonstrating that the training is transferrable beyond the HBCU.

Not having 'weed out' courses does not make an institution easy or "slower-track." It makes the institution more responsive to the students and more amenable to the demands of the labor market.

DEBUNKING THE BS ABOUT BLACK COLLEGES

HBCUs have a rich history and powerful mystique that continues to shape African American culture and inspire academic success. In popular culture, HBCUs have provided the context for movies, such as School Daze and Drumline, and television series, such as A Different World and The Quad. As one of many higher education options, HBCUs have also been subject to fair and unfair scrutiny from education consumers, policymakers, cultural critics, and social commentators. Many people who critique HBCUs base their opinions on speculation, biases, and myths. Using IPEDS and other studies, I explain other points people often get wrong about HBCUs.

Myth 1: HBCUs Have a Declining Enrollment

The total enrollment of HBCUs has continued to make steady gains over the last two decades. According to the most recent data from IPEDS, the total enrollment of HBCUs collectively is 311,671, compared to 260,749 in 1990. Seventy-nine of the 105 HBCUs surveyed have a larger enrollment today than they did in 1990. Only 26 HBCUs have experienced enrollment declines since 1990, with percentage drops ranging from 1 percent to 55 percent. Twelve HBCUs lost more than 20 percent of their student population when comparing their enrollment of 2012 with their enrollment in 1990. In 2013, three HBCUs had an enrollment of more than 10,000 students. There are 31 HBCUs with an enrollment of fewer than 1,000 students. While student enrollment is generally regarded as a positive indicator for the school, the ideal size for a university varies. Therefore, enrollment gains or losses over time are a more reliable indicator of the institution's health.

161

Myth 2: HBCUs Are Losing Enrollment because More Black Students Are Choosing Predominately White Institutions

Although most HBCUs have grown enrollment since 1990 (see response to Myth 1), the data also reveals that the total gain in HBCU attendance has not outpaced the gains made in Black students attending institutions of higher education generally. However, HBCUs are not losing a lot of students to PWIs. HBCUs are generally more selective than they were ten years ago and are losing students to open admissions community and for-profit colleges.

Over the past decade, state laws or board policies have restricted admissions at traditional 4-year colleges based on the idea that students who are less academically prepared should begin their postsecondary matriculation at community colleges. These changes include setting a minimum ACT or SAT requirement for public universities or prohibiting public 4-year colleges from offering remedial classes. In tandem, some private HBCUs have lost enrollment because of governance issues and difficulties marketing the tuition against more affordable higher education options. Sixty-five of the 101 HBCUs that qualify for Federal Student Financial Aid have selective admissions, while the remaining 36 campuses have open admissions. Only four of the 34 open admissions HBCUs are public.

Myth 3: HBCUs Have Low Graduation Rates

The average graduation rate for students across all 4-year HBCUs is 42 percent. That rate or percentage is slightly above the graduation rate for Black students at all institutions, but less than half the rate of the most selective PWIs. The three universities with the highest graduation rates for Black students within six years are Yale, Harvard, and Princeton. For HBCUs, the top three are Spelman College, Howard University, and Hampton University.

However, analyses that evaluate the success of colleges and universities by observing their 6-year cohort graduation rate can be elusive. On the surface, graduation rates tell us little about a college's or university's ability to educate a racially and economically diverse student body. Of the 23 colleges and universities in the nation that have a graduation rate for Black students that is in the 90s, the average annual cost of tuition and fees is $43,700 and the average percent of the student body that is Pell eligible is 15 percent. By contrast only five HBCUs have an annual tuition that is greater than $20,000, and the average percent of the total HBCU enrollment that is Pell eligible is 72.8 percent. In short, HBCU graduation rates reflect the chances they take to educate low income students, not the quality of education they provide.

Myth 4: HBCUs Have Low Endowments

The average endowment across HBCUs that participate in Federal Title IV funding is $27.7 million. Seven HBCUs have endowments that exceed $100 million: Howard University, Spelman College, Hampton University, Xavier University of Louisiana, Morehouse College, Meharry Medical College, and Tuskegee University. However, some HBCUs have lower than desired endowments and need financial support from stakeholders. Fourteen 4-year HBCUs have endowments that are less than $2 million, or less than 1 percent of the average endowment for all HBCUs.

Myth 5: The Ratio of Females-to-Males at HBCUs Is Something
Ridiculous, like 15-to-1

"It's not uncommon to have an HBCU with a 20:1 female/male ratio. How does anyone hear these numbers w/o flipping out? It can't get worse."

This was a September 15, 2013 tweet by noted educational commentator, Dr. Steve Perry. Janks Morton received similar responses when he asked students at Howard University, "What is the female-to-male ratio here?" for his documentary *Hoodwinked*. Many Black people believe that Black males are gradually disappearing, not only from HBCUs, but from higher education in general.

Contrary to popular belief, according to the Integrated Postsecondary Education Data System (IPEDS), the current ratio of Black females to Black males at HBCUs is less than 2-to-1 (1.57-to-1 to be exact). Across the 311,671 students who currently attend HBCUs, 121,414 are male and 190,257 are female. Coppin State University is the most skewed at 3.5-to-1. Almost 20 percent (19.5%) of all co-ed HBCUs have either an even split or has more males than females. For the three single gender schools, Morehouse has nearly as many males as the combined female population of Spelman College and Bennett College (U.S. Department of Education's National Center for Education Statistics, 2018).

Myth 6: HBCUs Offer a Substandard Education and Many Have
Accreditation Issues

As previously stated, when it comes to producing Black graduates who go on to earn Ph.D.'s, HBCUs compete successfully with the nation's best universities, including Ivy League universities, elite private colleges, and flagship state universities. Research also demonstrates that HBCU graduates enjoy greater financial success in their careers, and U.S. rankings consistently show that HBCUs are among the top producers of students who continue their educations through graduate and professional schools. My research indicates that for black students, HBCUs are clearly superior to predominantly white institutions for promoting positive student-faculty relationships and students' sense of belonging among science, technology, engineering, and mathematics majors.

Most HBCUs are advancing. Eighteen HBCUs have improved their Carnegie Classification within the last ten years, and only five of 101 currently have issues with their accreditation. Many HBCUs have formal recognition for having a robust research infrastructure. Howard University, Jackson State University, Clark Atlanta University, North Carolina A & T, and Florida A & M are all classified as High Research Activity. Seven HBCUs have a Carnegie Classification of 17 (DRU: Doctoral/Research Universities) – Prairie View A & M University; Texas Southern University; University of Maryland Eastern Shore; Bowie State University; Morgan State University; South Carolina State University; and Tennessee State University.

Among HBCUs that have a Carnegie Classification of "Doctoral Granting Research University," the percent of the faculty that is Black or African American is 67%. By contrast, the percentage of the faculty at doctoral granting Traditionally White Institutions (TWI) that is Black is 4%.

HBCUS AND STEM

Historically Black colleges and universities (HBCUs) share a common mission to provide and increase educational opportunities for underserved communities, and are uniquely positioned to increase the pipeline of Black students who go on to pursue advanced degrees and careers in STEM. Although HBCUs represent 3% of the nation's institutions of higher learning, they remain among the nation's top baccalaureate-origin institutions for a significant proportion of African American S&E doctoral recipients (Fiegener & Proudfoot, 2013). In 2010, the National Research Council noted the effectiveness of HBCUs in increasing participation and success of minority students in S&E fields, evidenced by their ability to graduate a larger percentage of African American students than PWIs (National Research Council, 2010).

Further research is necessary to answer a simple, yet very important question: How do HBCUs, which generally have smaller enrollments and fewer resources, achieve success in graduating Black students who earn doctorates in S&E at a pace only observed among the nation's Research 1 (R1) institutions? Obvious institutional characteristics, such as size and research designation, do not distinguish HBCUs that appear on the NSF list from HBCUs and PWIs that did not. Therefore, research is necessary for national efforts to reveal unique factors associated with diversifying the S&E workforce, that have only been observed in HBCUs of diverse Carnegie classifications and a uniform group PWIs comprised mostly of R1 institutions.

LINKAGE TO THEORY AND RESEARCH

A *2014 Historically Black Colleges and Universities Data Dashboard* report from the White House Initiative on HBCUs summarized assets and challenges of HBCUs generally across a broad cross-section of institutional variables (Toldson & Cooper, 2014). The HBCU Dashboard study found variance between HBCUs' enrollment patterns, retention and graduation rates, funding from competitive grants and contracts, state allocations, donations, endowments, tenures of administrative heads, administrative vacancies, percentage of tenured faculty members, faculty salaries, and accreditation. The variance in these characteristics could distinguish between HBCUs that appeared on the NSF Top 50 list and those that did not.

In addition, Toldson and Esters (2012) used the Minority Male STEM Initiative (MMSI Campus Survey) to develop a theory of change to understand factors associated with HBCUs' success in graduating students in STEM (Esters & Toldson, 2013). The purpose of the MMSI Campus Survey was to understand how university administrators, STEM faculty, and students of color in STEM disciplines navigate the path to recruiting, retaining, and graduating underrepresented students in STEM disciplines. A group of national scholars assembled by Association of Public and Land-grant Universities (APLU) staff developed the survey instrument, which was subsequently distributed to universities participating in the study and published in reports and peer-reviewed publications (Esters & Toldson, 2013; Toldson, 2013).

Factor analysis of the survey responses revealed three factors: (a) faculty relationships, (b) belonging, and (c) academic pressure. Using regression estimates, a factor score was assigned to each participant, which were used to compare means across institution types. Results indicated that students at HBCUs were significantly more likely than students at PWIs to have better relationships with faculty and to have a higher sense of "belonging."

Other recent studies on HBCUs' production of STEM graduates reveal a myriad of factors that provide a theoretical basis for exploring the institutional and student characteristics. Specific findings include:

HBCUs Have a Unique Structure That Could Foster a More Supportive Environment for STEM Students

Studies indicate that the mentoring that occurs naturally from HBCU faculty having higher teaching loads and more contact with undergraduate students can evince positive outcomes for HBCU STEM students (Kendricks, Nedunuri, & Arment, 2013). The number of faculty members of color at HBCUs, specifically Black faculty members (Jett, 2013) that understood Black culture (Gasman & Nguyen, 2016; Toldson, 2013), has also been cited as a factor that enhanced mentoring and student success at HBCUs in the existing literature.

HBCUs Have Developed Policies and Practices to Accommodate and Advance STEM Students with Less Academic Preparation and Resources

HBCUs educate a cross-section of STEM students, including first-generation college students and community college transfers (Jackson, 2013; Smith, 2016). Through a meta-synthesis, one study investigated HBCUs' role in preparing first-generation STEM students and found that several unique components of the HBCU STEM learning environment include: assessing prior academic performance; facilitating college adjustment; social integration; and academic socialization (Hicks & Wood, 2016).

Another study demonstrated how some HBCUs use "retention theories" to retain lesser prepared STEM students through interviews with STEM program coordinators at HBCUs (Palmer, Davis, & Thompson, 2010). Based on research linking retention to early academic placement and experiences, HBCUs survey focused on helping students test out of remedial mathematics and English courses, through mandatory tutoring, research, and critical thinking training. Another study also found that HBCUs provide early supports for underrepresented STEM students to help mitigate the challenges presented by mathematics as an access point for STEM entry (Adams, Robinson, Covington, & Talley-Matthews, 2017), including through summer bridge programs (Fakayode, Yakubu, Adeyeye, Pollard, & Mohammed, 2014). These types of supports have shown to effectively facilitate the progress of HBCUs STEM students.

*HBCUs Use of Culturally Relevant Pedagogical Approaches Foster the
Academic Success of STEM Students*

Several research studies postulate that HBCUs advance STEM education
among African American students because of the connection between
racial identity development (Brown, Mangram, Sun, Cross, & Raab,
2017), critical race theory (Adams et al., 2017; Lundy-Wagner, 2013) and
Black student achievement. These studies reinforce the impact of shared
cultural experiences, understanding the role of racism and discrimination
on opportunities, and the socio-cognitive benefits of being exposed to
highly educated Black people. According to IPEDS, among HBCUs that
have a Carnegie Classification of "Doctoral-Granting Research University,"
the percent of the faculty that is Black or African American is 67%. By
contrast, the percentage of Black faculty at doctoral-granting traditionally
White institutions (TWI) is 4%. Intersectional issues associated with Black
women and Black men in STEM at HBCUs have also been observed (Perna
et al., 2009).

Conclusions

The literature highlights many unifying features that appear to be related to
HBCUs successfully preparing and graduating underrepresented minority
students in STEM. However, there are many unanswered questions.
For instance, many of these studies observed the normal practices and
policies of HBCUs, without clearly indicating if the practices occurred
naturally because of African American cultural nuances, or strategically
to accommodate their students. In addition, analyses of institutional and
student characteristics reveal vast diversity among HBCUs' institutional
characteristics (Simms & Bock, 2014). It is not completely clear whether
variation in the success of HBCUs is a function of lack of knowledge transfer
between institutions, or because of resource differences between the higher-
performing HBCUs and the HBCUs with lower performance levels. Further
research is necessary to help us to distill the unique student and institutional
characteristics that are associated with HBCUs successfully preparing and
graduating STEM students.

The insights gleaned from the literature helps us to further refine a
theory of change to elucidate the trajectory that is necessary for HBCUs to
successfully graduate future scientists. Specifically, further research should
be intentional about looking for unique environmental structures associated

with mentoring and STEM success. In addition, researchers should pay careful attention to specific HBCU's policies and practices to accommodate students with less academic preparation and financial resources. Finally, further research should explore how the cultural context of students' educational and professional experiences impact their matriculation in STEM disciplines at HBCUs.

BELIEVING IN HBCUS

For more than 150 years, HBCUs have made historic and continuing contributions to the general welfare and prosperity of our country, and serve as engines for economic growth. These institutions, which today serve more than 300,000 undergraduate and graduate students, have enabled men and women of all ethnic, racial, and economic backgrounds, especially African Americans, to assume leadership and service roles in their communities.

Most of America's civil rights giants were educated at HBCUs – Dr. King, W.E.B. DuBois, Rosa Parks, Booker T. Washington, and Thurgood Marshall. In our time, Jesse Jackson, Andy Young, Barbara Jordan, Congressman John Lewis, Marian Wright Edelman, and Doug Wilder all earned their degrees at HBCUs. Legendary artists and authors came out of HBCUs – Ralph Ellison, Alice Walker, Zora Neale Hurston, Langston Hughes, and Toni Morrison. Even though our nation's HBCUs make up just 3 percent of colleges and universities, they produce 27 percent of African American students with bachelor's degrees in STEM fields and one-fourth of the bachelor's degrees in education awarded to African-Americans.

Notwithstanding HBCUs' success over several generations, many HBCUs have experienced financial hardships and administrative challenges. I do not challenge the myths associated with HBCUs to minimize legitimate concerns, rather to provide the best information to HBCU advocates who are genuinely interested in promoting HBCU growth and sustainability. Many detractors have used misinformation about HBCUs question the relevancy of HBCUs.

Using myths and misinformation to question the relevancy of HBCUs is not new. Several years ago, I met the legendary president of Xavier University, Norman Francis. He told me that the year he became president of Xavier in 1968, someone asked him if HBCUs were still necessary. For HBCUs to achieve greatness, they must relinquish the posture of defending their relevance and get in the stance of asserting their excellence.

65 YEARS AFTER BROWN V. BOARD OF EDUCATION: HOW IMPORTANT IS INTEGRATION? – AN AFTERTHOUGHT

It should be against the law to deny anybody access to a school based on race, and Brown versus the Board of Education achieved that for us. But if we stick to a narrative that suggests that predominantly Black schools are inherently going to be bad, and that's why we need integration, we're setting our children up for failure.

We've tried forced busing. We've tried forced integration. The results have too often been White flight, school district secessions, and re-segregation through various alternatives to public schools. Even successfully integrated schools have challenges. Anytime we have schools that are 20 percent Black, but 60 percent of the suspensions are Black, and within-school segregation where the special education program is almost all Black and the honors classes are all White, there's still a problem.

While the presence of a diverse student population is desirable, it is not absolutely necessary to, nor is it independently an effective means to, achieve educational equity. What is necessary is for every student, regardless of the composition of their school, to get the same amount of resources and the same amount of attention to the curriculum and pedagogy that best suits their needs.

We need great predominantly Black schools. We need great integrated schools. If we make predominantly Black schools excellent, we're going to see a natural transformation in the Black community, and in our society.

BEING AN HBCU SCHOLAR

In the summer of 2008, as an assistant professor at Howard University, I spent a week at the UNC – Chapel Hill as a member of a program designed to mentor junior faculty. During the program, an older White female university administrator reviewed my resume. She spoke of the pride she took in mentoring faculty members of color through the academy.

During our session, she shook her head and said:

You're in big trouble. Your research is all over the place. There's no rhyme or reason to your activities, and you're participating in too many things that have nothing to do with you getting tenure. Trust me, I've seen this scenario play out too many times. The university will use you for the exposure you're giving them from your community and civic activity, but they will never reward you with tenure. You really need to focus your work on ONE key topic area, and only work toward getting published in peer-reviewed journals and getting grants.

My jaw dropped. I really didn't know what to say, but my first thought was, "THANK GOD I teach at an HBCU!"

Although she didn't give me advice I could use, she did give me a greater appreciation for my station. Only eight years later, I not only achieved tenure, but was promoted to the rank of full professor while on leave from Howard to serve President Obama's administration.

REFERENCES

Adams, T., Robinson, D., Covington, A., & Talley-Matthews, S. (2017). Fueling the STEMM pipeline: How historically Black colleges and universities improve the presence of African American scholars in STEMM. *Journal of Urban Learning, Teaching, and Research, 13,* 9–25.

Brown, B. A., Mangram, C., Sun, K., Cross, K., & Raab, E. (2017). Representing racial identity: Identity, race, the construction of the African American STEM students. *Urban Education, 52*(2), 170–206.

Esters, L. L., & Toldson, I. A. (2013). Supporting minority male education in Science, Technology, Engineering, and Mathematics (STEM) disciplines. *Texas Education Review, 1,* 209–219.

Fakayode, S. O., Yakubu, M., Adeyeye, O. M., Pollard, D. A., & Mohammed, A. K. (2014). Promoting undergraduate STEM education at a historically Black college and university through research experience. *Journal of Chemical Education, 91*(5), 662–665.

Fiegener, M. K., & Proudfoot, S. L. (2013). *Baccalaureate origins of U.S.-trained S & E doctorate recipients.* Retrieved from http://www.nsf.gov/statistics/infbrief/nsf13323/nsf13323.pdf

Gasman, M., & Nguyen, T.-H. (2016). Engaging voices: Methods for studying STEM education at Historically Black Colleges and Universities (HBCUs). *Journal for Multicultural Education, 10*(2), 194–205.

Hicks, T., & Wood, J. L. (2016). A meta-synthesis of academic and social characteristic studies: First-generation college students in STEM disciplines at HBCUs. *Journal for Multicultural Education, 10*(2), 107–123.

Jackson, D. L. (2013). A balancing act: Impacting and initiating the success of African American female community college transfer students in STEM into the HBCU environment. *Journal of Negro Education, 82*(3), 255–271. doi:10.7709/jnegroeducation.82.3.0255

Jett, C. (2013). HBCUs propel African American male mathematics majors. *Journal of African American Studies, 17*(2), 189–205. doi:10.1007/s12111-011-9194-x

Kendricks, K. D., Nedunuri, K. V., & Arment, A. R. (2013). Minority student perceptions of the impact of mentoring to enhance academic performance in STEM disciplines. *Journal of STEM Education: Innovations and Research, 14*(2), 38–46.

Lundy-Wagner, V. C. (2013). Is it really a man's world? Black men in science, technology, engineering, and mathematics at historically Black colleges and universities. *Journal of Negro Education, 82*(2), 157–168.

National Center for Education Statistics. (2015). *The Integrated Postsecondary Education Data System (IPEDS)*. Retrieved January 16, 2015, from http://nces.ed.gov/ipeds/

National Research Council. (2010). *Expanding underrepresented minority participation: America's science and technology talent at the crossroads.* Washington, DC: National Research Council.

Palmer, R. T., Davis, R. J., & Thompson, T. (2010). Theory meets practice: HBCU initiatives that promote academic success among African Americans in STEM. *Journal of College Student Development, 51*(4), 440–443.

Perna, L., Lundy-Wagner, V., Drezner, N. D., Gasman, M., Yoon, S., Bose, E., & Gary, S. (2009). The contribution of HBCUS to the preparation of African American women for stem careers: A case study. *Research in Higher Education, 50*(1), 1–23. doi:10.1007/s11162-008-9110-y

Simms, K., & Bock, S. (2014). Are Historically Black Colleges and Universities (HBCUs) in the United States a single institutional group? Evidence from educational outcomes. *Education Research and Perspectives, 41*(1), 115–129.

Smith, D. J. (2016). Operating in the middle: The experiences of African American female transfer students in STEM degree programs at HBCUs. *Community College Journal of Research and Practice, 40*(12), 1025–1039.

Toldson, I. A. (2013). Historically Black colleges and universities can promote leadership and excellence in STEM (Editor's commentary). *Journal of Negro Education, 82*(4), 359–367. doi:10.7709/jnegroeducation.82.4.0359

Toldson, I. A., & Cooper, G. (2014). *Historically Black colleges and universities data dashboard.* Washington, DC: The White House Initiative on Historically Black Colleges and Universities.

BELIEVING IN BLACK STUDENTS

*Black students need us to tell them about their potential to be great,
rather than warning them of their risks for failure.*

***

When something doesn't go your way, you've just got to adjust. You've
got to dig deep and work like crazy, and that's when you'll find out
what you're really made of during those hard times, but you can only
do that if you're willing to put yourself in a position where you might
fail, and that's why so often failure is the key to success.

– Michelle Obama (2013)

Michelle Obama said this during a graduation speech for Martin Luther King
Jr. Academic Magnet High School in Nashville, Tennessee (Saenz, 2013).
Obama used several examples of people, including her husband President
Barack Obama and Oprah Winfrey, to illustrate that triumph is a natural
byproduct of adversity.

Many Black students persist in an environment that often feels unwelcoming.
Studies show that Black students are more likely to attend schools in a high
security environment and less likely to perceive care and respect from their
teachers (Toldson, 2008). In addition, most Black high school graduates have
had to adapt to a racially biased curriculum that undermines their culture's
contribution to any field. Within this context, educators have a unique
opportunity to impart wisdom and inspire postsecondary success among
Black students, by reaffirming Black culture and helping Black students
create a personal narrative of success.

Unfortunately, many educators and advocates use BS to denigrate and
dispirit Black students through a mind-numbing recital of poorly sourced
statistics, which imply that, for example, Black students have a better
chance of going to prison than to college and have a corrupt value system
that attributes being smart to "acting White." These types of condemnations
elicit a variety of emotions from students, ranging from boredom to unease.
Students who internalize such messages often conclude that the only path

to success is to distance themselves from their peers, community, and even their culture.

In this concluding chapter, I offer suggestions to educators, including teachers, administrators, advocates and parents, who have the attentive ear of one, or more, of our nations' Black students.

Embrace Chaos, Because Black Children Are Unpredictable

For more than a century, scientists have tried and failed to create a range of metrics designed to predict behaviors and outcomes for children. Widespread unqualified use of IQ and achievement testing, as well as social barometers, such as zip codes, poverty levels, and household compositions, have resulted in children being labeled "at risk," and tracked. However, despite relentless attempts by adults to measure the immeasurable, the exceptional child is not the exception, but the norm.

Understanding the delicate balance between insight and scientific observations is key to educating in a diverse context. Great educators are not dependent on metrics that are designed for social control. They are visionaries who can see something extraordinary in the ordinary. Great educators do not rely on deducing experiences and prognosticating based on superficial observations; they induce with a mix of art, science, and spirit to expand their purview of possibilities for children.

Chaos theory reveals the deceptively small incidents that cause major events; like the flapping of a butterfly's wings causing a hurricane in a distant land. In that view many small immeasurable things that we experience with our students can evoke memories, sensations, and actions that can change the world. This book aims to help us appreciate the chaos that exists in our educational settings, while developing the knowledge and skills to teach and learn, think and feel, and be reasonable and have faith.

Black Children Need to Understand Their Greatness

Recently, I asked a group of teachers and school administrators if their Black students would be more inclined to revere General Andrew Jackson or General Garson. Most of them had not heard of General Garson. General Garson was a free Black man who was the commander of a British outpost known as the "Negro Fort" on Prospect Bluff in Spanish Florida in 1814. After the War of 1812, British troops left the fort to General Garson and a militia of about 400 Black militiamen. From the outpost, General Garson provided refuge to Africans who escaped from plantations in Georgia, Alabama, and South Carolina. Eventually, the militia organized attacks on plantations to rescue other Africans held in slavery. After much angst among southern plantation owners, Andrew Jackson illegally sent troops into Spanish-occupied Florida to attack the fort, killing at least 200 free Black men, including General Garson by firing squad (Riordan, 1996).

One must acknowledge the humanity of Black and native people to understand that the battle between General Garson and General Jackson, along with the ensuing Seminole Wars, was a civil war, not unlike the War Between the States. This is only one among hundreds of lessons omitted from Black students' curricula. True American history involves Black people making a material contribution to the development of this nation as well as to the liberation of Black people, often through armed resistance and social diplomacy.

Contrarily, Black students are constantly confronted with a cultural mythology in education that embraces historical figures who were complicit in victimizing their ancestors, against a faded backdrop of Black victims, bystanders, and a few isolated Black protagonists. One of my students for life, a gifted conscious hip-hop artist from Oklahoma named Marcel P. Black once told me that he left home to attend college at Southern University before he learned of his home states' legacy of "Black Wall Street." He firmly believed that if he and his peers learned their history in school, more of them would have aspired to greatness. Educators can help Black students realize their prominence by revealing rich information about their legacy. If we want Black students to be serious about education, we need to be serious about educating them about who they are.

Black Children Need Help Defining Themselves for Themselves

During an in-service training for staff members of a public high school, I asked the participants to describe the neighborhoods of their students. I heard phrases like "crime-ridden," "broken homes," and "drug-infested." I then asked if anyone grew up in neighborhoods that were similar to their students.' After several raised their hands, I asked, "How did you grow up in such a neighborhood and still become successful?" This question spurred a more meaningful dialogue about inner-city neighborhoods that considered community assets, hope and resilience, against a more measured examination of community challenges.

Black graduates are keenly aware of the problems facing the Black community. They are less clear about how to capitalize on the unique

175

opportunities for character building, leadership, and civic engagement that germinates in imperfect living situations. This concept is very difficult for many to grasp who have grown up without struggle. For example, after I told a group of school administrators in a large metro area that they have to impart success within the context of their students' environment; one participant suggested that I was promoting lower standards for Black students. She assumed that a "standard" that is unique to the Black community is, in essence, "lower." To the contrary, the standard I was suggesting is much higher.

Western culture imposes a value on avoiding problem behaviors and disconnecting from undesirable circumstances. This is reflected in the rather guileless advice we give to teenagers to "stay away from the wrong crowd" – a near impossible objective for children in densely populated communities. Few Black students from tough environments will define success in terms of isolating themselves from their peers to prepare themselves for a distant agenda. A standard of success for most Black youth would be to influence their peers rather than avoid them, and work to better their communities rather than disconnecting from them. In this view, assessing their success through standardized tests is impossible. The standards of success for many Black students are learning with purpose, applying knowledge to the real world, creative problem solving, and verbal acumen. Therefore, when a Black student asks, "What does this have to do with me?" when confronted with a difficult subject in school, they genuinely need an accurate response. Educators can help Black students redefine their personal and cultural standards of success, so that education can become less passive and abstract, and more affirming and relevant.

Black Students Need to See Us for Who We Really Are

I had the honor of sharing a panel with Raymond Lucas, a youth development nonprofit executive, and president of the 100 Black Men of Maryland. I was honored when he told the audience that my research influenced him to revise his speeches to Black students. He said that he abandoned the trite statistics and chose to focus on what motivated him to beat the odds. This strategy helped him to develop a deeper connection with his listeners.

I also use this strategy. I once delivered a keynote address entitled, "You Have the Right to Remain Educated," for the Wisconsin Association of Black Men at the University of Wisconsin. About twenty Black male teenagers from Urban Prep Academies traveled from Chicago to participate in the program. After my speech, a senior at Urban Prep enthusiastically embraced me and said, "I go to church every Sunday, and I've never felt like this … You woke up something in me, and I'm ready to be heard!" I was elated that my words inspired him to tell his own story.

In many ways, we are selected to speak to Black students for all the wrong reasons. Our material success gives people the illusion that our lives are, and always has been, perfect. To the contrary, most of us who have achieved success have endured many uncertain, disorderly and painful periods. However, as quantum scientists suggest, chaos is the natural order of life, from which all things perfect spring forth. In that view, the mission of a speaker is not to impose order on imperfect lives, but to clarify the very essence of success.

As Michelle Obama said, "Often, failure is the key to success." I was designated a "slow learner" in the fourth grade. I graduated from a public high school in Baton Rouge, Louisiana, that was marred in drugs and violence during a significant portion of my high school years. I consistently scored within the 20th percentile or less on every standardized test I took, including the ACT and the GRE. However, I am not successful despite the blemishes of his past, but because of them.

Black Children Need Us to Invest in Them

Whether you are having a personal conversation or working with an educator, activist, politician, foundation or corporation, understand the difference between people who are working to solve problems and people who are investing in problems.

Problem solvers:

- Actively work to find solutions and regularly use good data to measure and evaluate evidence of progress.
- May not know precisely the solution but is optimistic about progress and change.
- Have a clear perspective of their identity and utility beyond the problem and is eager to move on to a new agenda once the problem is solved.

People who are invested in a problem:

- Spend more time trying to convince others of the magnitude of the problem, often relying on BS, and less time trying to solve the problem.
- Are usually pessimistic and skeptical of any information that suggests the problem is improving.

- Have a personal or professional identity that is connected to the problem, and have difficulty demonstrating their value in the absence of the problem. Study and understand problems associated with educating Black children, but never invest in them. Use good data, thoughtful analyses, and a compassionate understanding to invest in Black children's future.

REFERENCES

Riordan, P. (1996). Finding freedom in Florida: Native peoples, African Americans, and colonists, 1670–1816. *The Florida Historical Quarterly, 75,* 24–43.

Ruggles, S., Alexander, J. T., Genadek, K., Goeken, R., Schroeder, M. B., & Sobek, M. (2012). *Integrated public use microdata series: Version 5.0* [Machine-readable database]. Minneapolis, MN: University of Minnesota.

Saenz, A. (2013). *Michelle Obama makes light of president's failures in graduation speech.* Retrieved from http://abcnews.go.com/blogs/politics/2013/05/michelle-obama-makes-light-of-presidents-failures-in-graduation-speech/

Toldson, I. A. (2008). *Breaking barriers: Plotting the path to academic success for school-age African-American males.* Washington, DC: Congressional Black Caucus Foundation.

Toldson, I. A., & Esters, L. L. (2012). *The quest for excellence: Supporting the academic success of minority males in Science, Technology, Engineering, and Mathematics (STEM) disciplines.* Washington, DC: Association of Public and Land-grant Universities.

ABOUT THE AUTHOR

Ivory A. Toldson, Ph.D., is a professor of Counseling Psychology at Howard University, the president of Quality Education for Minorities, the editor-in-chief of the *Journal of Negro Education*, and executive editor of the *Journal of Policy Analysis and Research*, published by the Congressional Black Caucus Foundation, Inc.

Dr. Toldson began his career at Southern University, where he was awarded the W.E.B. DuBois Fellowship from the United States Department of Justice for his research on police psychology. He also wrote Black Sheep: When the American Dream Becomes a Black Man's Nightmare, a novel for which he won the EboNetwork's Changing Faces award.

Dr. Toldson was previously appointed by President Barack Obama to be the executive director of the White House Initiative on Historically Black Colleges and Universities. In this position, he worked with the U.S. Secretary of Education to devise national strategies to sustain and expand federal support to HBCUs.

As contributing education editor for *The Root*, Dr. Toldson gained a national reputation for debunking myths about African-Americans and challenging what he considers "BS," or Bad Stats. For most of his research he uses data analytics to contextualize and refute, commonly held notions about barriers to African American progress. He had a prominent role in Janks Morton's documentary, Hoodwinked. Because of his reputation as a "myth buster," he routinely interviews for *PolitiFact*, where he critiqued claims made by Ben Carson, President Jimmy Carter and Sen. John Eichelberger.

Dr. Toldson was dubbed a leader "who could conceivably navigate the path to the White House" by the *Washington Post*, one of "30 leaders in the fight for Black men," by *Newsweek Magazine*, and the "Problem Solver" by *Diverse: Issues in Higher Education*. Dr. Toldson has also been featured on MSNBC, C-SPAN2, NPR News and numerous national and local radio stations. In print, his research has been featured in *The Washington Post*, *CNN.com*, *The New York Times*, *The National Journal*, *Essence Magazine*, *BET.com*, *The Grio*, and *Ebony Magazine*.

Dr. Toldson was named in The Root 100, an annual ranking of the most influential African-American leaders. He was awarded the: Equity Champion Award from the New York City Department of Education; Outstanding Alumni Award from Penn State Black Alumni Association; an LSU Legend by the LSU Black Alumni Chapter; and one of the Top 25 Forensic Psychology Professors from ForensicsColleges.com. Since 2016, as QEM president, Dr. Toldson has served as principal investigator of 8 National Science Foundation awards, totaling more than $3.2 million, to support capacity building efforts for STEM programs at Minority Serving Institutions.

Dr. Toldson received a B.S. in psychology from Louisiana State University, an M.Ed. in counseling from the Pennsylvania State University, and a Ph.D. in counseling psychology from Temple University. He was awarded a Doctor of Humane Letters from Florida Memorial University at their 137th commencement in 2016.

Dr. Toldson is married to Marshella Toldson, and together, they are raising their daughter, Makena, and son, Ivory Kaleb, in Washington, DC.

Made in the USA
Columbia, SC
05 August 2021

GARLiC
& the
WiTCH

GaRLiC

& the

WiTCH

BRee PauLsen

Quill Tree Books
Imprints of HarperCollinsPublishers

ISBN 978-0-06-299512-4 (TRADE BDG.)

ISBN 978-0-06-299511-7 (PBK.)

THE ARTIST USED ADOBE PHOTOSHOP AND PROCREATE TO CREATE THE DIGITAL ILLUSTRATIONS

FOR THIS BOOK.

TYPOGRAPHY BY DAVID CURTIS

23 24 25 26   RTLO   10 9 8 7 6 5 4 3 2

❖

FIRST EDITION

TO ALL THE SPROUTS
FACING BIG CHANGES AND UNCERTAINTY

chapter one

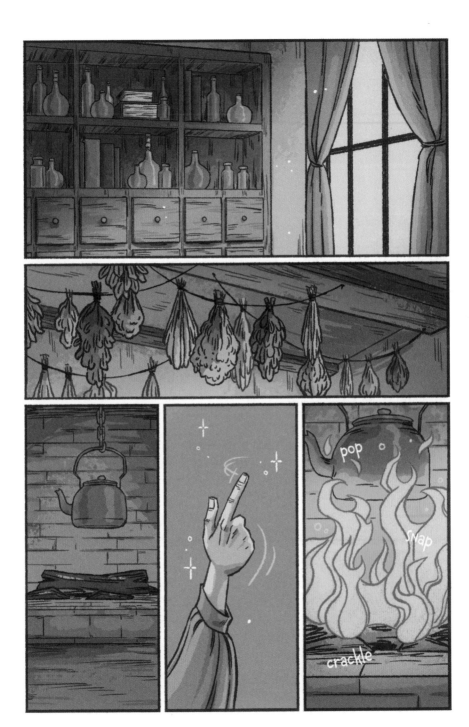

pop

snap

crackle

3

4

8

9

NOW, LET'S SEE...

I DON'T NEED THAT MUCH.

ABOUT A QUARTER SHOULD DO, I THINK.

OH, I HOPE THIS WORKS.

WELL...

creak

...IT WAS WORTH A TRY.

thump

rump

bump

chapter two

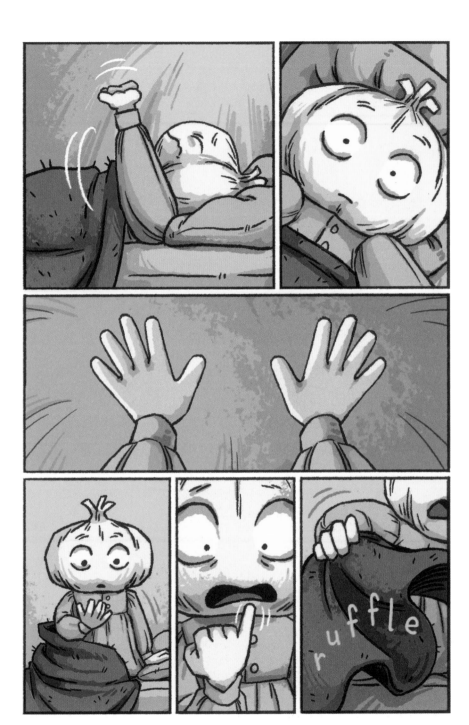

25

29

HMM, HE'S PROBABLY IN THE GREENHOUSE.

YOU JUST MISSED AGNES.

SHE DROPPED OFF A NEW BLEND OF HERBS FOR MY BLOOD SUBSTITUTE POTION.

GRAPES, SHE WAS HERE?

I HAVE A QUESTION FOR HER...OH WELL, MAYBE I'LL VISIT HER LATER.

NOW, LET'S SEE IF WE FINALLY GOT IT.

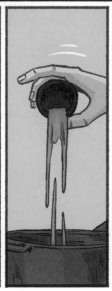

Sip

HMM...

STILL NOT QUITE RIGHT.

I'M SURE WE'LL GET IT RIGHT SOON.

WE ARE DEFINITELY GETTING CLOSE.

I CAN FEEL IT.

CARROT THINKS IT MEANS I'M GOING TO TURN HUMAN.

THAT'D BE EXCITING!

HAVE YOU SHOWN AGNES?

NOT YET...

I GATHER YOU AREN'T EXCITED ABOUT THIS POSSIBILITY.

WELL, YEAH! IT'D BE A BIG CHANGE—

A BIG CHANGE I MAY NOT WANT!

THAT IS TRUE. BIG CHANGES CAN BE SCARY.

ANYWAY, I THINK YOU'D LIKE BEING HUMAN.

AND I'M SURE THE OTHERS WILL START CHANGING, TOO. YOU'LL HAVE EACH OTHER TO LEAN ON FOR SUPPORT.

I HOPE THAT IS THE CASE.

THIS WHOLE SITUATION WOULD BE A LOT LESS SCARY IF I DIDN'T HAVE TO GO THROUGH IT ALONE.

IT'D BE NICE TO HAVE CARROT BY MY SIDE.

EXACTLY!

OF COURSE, YOU WILL HAVE TO ASK AGNES IF YOU ARE **INDEED** TURNING INTO A HUMAN.

I KNOW, I JUST—

I DON'T WANT TO WASTE ANY OF HER TIME OVER THIS WHEN SHE HAS SO MUCH TO DO.

HEY, YOU WOULDN'T BE WASTING HER TIME.

IN FACT, I THINK SHE'D APPRECIATE THE BREAK TO CHAT WITH YOU.

SHE IS STILL TAKING THE TIME TO HELP ME OUT WHEN SHE DOESN'T HAVE TO.

SO DON'T LET YOUR FEAR OF BEING A BOTHER STOP YOU FROM REACHING OUT TO HER.

I GUESS YOU'RE RIGHT.

THANKS FOR HELPING ME WITH THIS.

OF COURSE, ANYTIME.

slide

chapter three

49

I DID FIND TIME TO FIGURE OUT A NEW HERB BLEND FOR COUNT, THOUGH!

YEAH, I WAS JUST AT THE CASTLE.

HE TRIED IT... AND IT WASN'T QUITE RIGHT.

OH...

I REALLY THOUGHT I'D FINALLY CRACKED IT.

EVEN FOUND MY MOTHER'S OLD NOTES FROM HER BLOOD SUBSTITUTE ATTEMPTS, BUT I GUESS I READ THEM WRONG—

DOESN'T HELP THAT HER SHORTHAND IS IMPOSSIBLE TO DECIPHER.

51

52

OKAY...

LET'S ASK HIM, THEN.

knock
knock

clk
clk
clk

AH! WITCH AGNES!

DID GARLIC TELL YOU ABOUT THE HERB BLEND?

THAT SETTLES IT, THEN.

YOU TWO CAN DEPART TOMORROW MORNING. THAT SHOULD GIVE YOU ENOUGH TIME TO PREPARE...

...AND GIVE ME TIME TO COMPILE A LIST OF ITEMS I'VE BEEN NEEDING.

THAT WORKS FOR ME! HOW ABOUT YOU, GARLIC?

YEAH, I'LL BE READY.

PERFECT! SEE YOU TOMORROW!

SEE YOU!

WELL, HOW EXCITING!

YOU GET TO GO ON A FUN LITTLE ADVENTURE, COUNT GETS THE MISSING INGREDIENT FOR HIS BLOOD SUBSTITUTE—

—AND I CAN FINALLY DO SOME MUCH-NEEDED RESTOCKING OF SOME HERBS AND SPICES!

?

GARLIC, IS THERE SOMETHING WRONG?

I DON'T KNOW WHAT IT MEANS.

IT MEANS YOU'RE GROWING.

GARLIC, SAY HELLO TO MY MOTHER.

HELLO...

THE WAY YOU TALK TO YOUR GARLIC TO HELP IT GROW IS MAGIC.

AND AS YOU GROW, YOU'LL BE ABLE TO DO MORE.

YOU COULD EVEN BRING YOUR OWN GARLIC BULBS TO LIFE IF YOU WANT TO.

SO IT WON'T JUST BE ME—

THE OTHERS WILL BECOME HUMAN TOO?

AT THEIR OWN PACE, BUT YES, ALL OF YOU WILL TAKE HUMAN FORM EVENTUALLY—

—WHICH MEANS I SHOULD INFORM THE OTHERS.

BUT I'LL TACKLE THAT LATER.

RIGHT NOW I NEED TO WRITE MY LIST AND MAKE PREPARATIONS FOR YOUR TRIP, AS SHOULD YOU.

GROW...

chapter four

tap

tap

tap

74

MORNING, CARROT!

MORNING!

MORNING, GARLIC!

HAVE FUN ON YOUR TRIP!

THANKS!

HEY, GARLIC!

WHAT DO YOU WANT, CELERY?

77

AH! MORNING! COME IN!

I'M JUST DOUBLE-CHECKING I WROTE DOWN EVERYTHING I NEED.

NOW, WHERE DID I PUT...

ARE WE GOING TO BE ABLE TO CARRY ALL THIS BACK?

NO, WHICH IS WHY I'VE WHIPPED UP THIS!

PLENTY OF SPACE IN HERE AND IT SHOULD STAY LIGHTWEIGHT.

BRILLIANT...

NOW, COUNT HAS BEEN TO THE MAGIC MARKET BEFORE, BUT JUST IN CASE—

I'VE ATTUNED THIS COMPASS TO ITS LOCATION SO YOU TWO WON'T GET LOST.

COOL.

NOW, THE BEST WAY TO GET THERE IS BY AIR—

COUNT, I ASSUME YOU WILL BE FLYING AS A BAT.

THAT IS CORRECT.

83

ALL RIGHT, ARE YOU READY FOR THE LAST LEG OF OUR JOURNEY?

YEAH!

WONDERFUL!

NOW, THE VALLEY WE'RE ABOUT TO ENTER HAS SOME WICKED WINDS—

—SO STAY CLOSE, OKAY?

OKAY.

poof

LET'S GO!

88

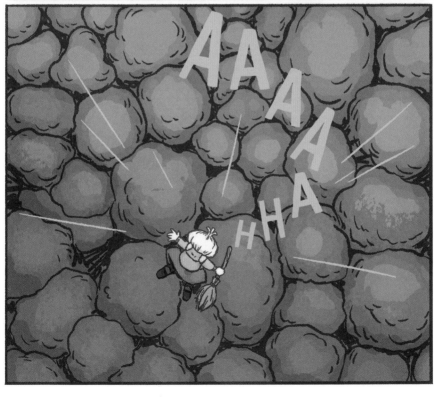

AAAAAHHA

chapter five

COUNT...

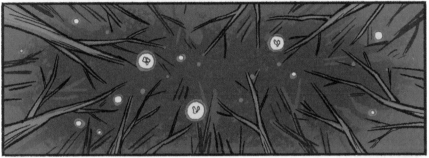

GARLIC?

COUNT!

GARLIC!

OH, THANK GOODNESS YOU'RE OKAY!

AND YOU USED THE COMPASS— GOOD!

YEAH!

I THOUGHT I'D HEAD TO THE MARKET IN HOPES OF MEETING YOU THERE.

I HOPED THE SAME.

110

112

WITCH
AGNES.

chapter six

122

HERE—

AND I'LL FIND A PLACE TO PLANT THE REST TO GROW MORE.

pat

pat

THIS SHOULD BE A GOOD SPOT.

GROW...

135

139

143

the end